The Road

MW01172451

THE 4C's

Civility, Community, Creativity, Climate Change

2nd Edition

Presented by

Dr. Anana Phifer - Derilhomme

TABLE OF CONTENTS

The 4C's was created to give young people especially girls and young women an opportunity to see themselves as the solution. Through this platform you will see the desire develop in others to want to make change and be the change. Once you put on your 4C colored glasses, you begin to see new opportunities for change.

There are 4 Principles of The 4 C's

Curiosity allows for investigation and exploration of the issues, questions and concerns of others. We allow the space for people to ask-"why or better yet why not?'.

Then it takes courage to ask the questions and don't stop until you get the answer. Mark Twain said "courage is resistance to fear, master of ear, not master of fear." Empowered youth will ask the tough question, make the tough decisions and do the tough jobs to achieve. Inquisitiveness is encouraged and celebrated when we work in the 4C. Doing things the "old way or just because we've done it like this for decades" is not an acceptable answer. Why do you do that? Why do you do it that way? Why do you do it at that time, at that location? All questions that sometimes we as adults may have not taken the time to consider. "Courage is moving forward in spite of fear." John C. Maxwell

Justina Mutale, an advocate for gender equality and the empowerment of women and girls, states in her book The Art of Iconic Leadership Power Secrets of Female World Leaders; "Creative leaders tend to think and act differently. They are courageous and curious." I couldn't agree more. It's one thing to have an idea that differs from others. It's another thing to take action and create movement around that idea. Imagine if our schools offered "Think Tanks" for young people to throw out creative ideas and solutions to problems? We would have a plethora of options and real solutions to implement and create sustainable change.

Create with the willingness to start where you are. Sometimes with nothing but an idea or a vision. What have you created lately? Or let's start with when was the last time you recognized or celebrated a creative achievement of someone or a concept that is already being implemented? Other times they take simple items like a pen and paper and create the vision by charting a roadmap for where they want to go. One of the most gratifying parts of being a mentor is seeing your mentee create their own and see the rewards and harvest of their work. Once they get it you see a level of gratitude and joy over take them. Simply, because they experienced their own dream or vision come true. As it happens once, they now have the faith that it can happen again. Not only can it happen again but they will grow in their faith and willingness to campaign for the change and experience it with their peers.

As we go down this road of sustainable change may you allow yourself to see and experience "The 4C Effect". As you read and continue on this journey may you join our campaign and walk alongside us on the road to sustainable change.

Fourth principle is to create a campaign for change. A new level of success with young people happens once they begin to campaign. In the end one's ability to organize and get to work on the goal is where the success lies. Be a champion for change. Pick a cause and stand for it. Fight for it.

It begins with curiosity. Curiosity to see if perhaps I can find the answer to a problem or if nothing else, lead the path or join the journey to a solution. As a youth empowerment leader I enjoy hearing youth ask me why. You see, challenging the status quo is what creates change and stimulates curiosity to find a better way of doing things. Once you get an idea or a vision you will need the courage to take the steps and move forward towards it, even if you have to walk alone. I proudly say that with BlessedGirls no one has to walk alone because our mentorship program gives each mentee access to a mentor that can help lead them and walk alongside them. It takes courage to stand up and stand out. I encourage our mentees to get comfortable with making courageous moves. Often I refer to taking your vitamin C in order to get through the day, especially those challenging days.

Through The 4C's we get to see how young people create. They sometimes take ideas and craft solutions.

The younger generations including Gen Z and Millennials have a unique perspective regarding the world, foreign policy, business and their future. I believe it takes ordinary people to do extraordinary things. Our children and young adults need the platform and direction to develop as leaders. Many teens want to lead, but have never been given the permission or the opportunity to do so.

A dynamic aspect of The 4C's is the power of choice. Many young adults believe they don't have a choice or believe their choices are limited. Everyone makes choices each and every day. I personally appreciate having choices. I understand people who prefer not to have to make a choice. The key aspect of a choice is the responsibility that comes with it. The responsibility to see it through and accept the consequences of your choices. Our youth make choices and with direction, education, support and inspiration they will make the right choices and reap great rewards. Under-privileged and at risk youth frequently make decisions out of desperation and what they consider limitations.

The mission of our platform is to get youth to be open to civility, kindness, respect and unity. Around the globe we see and hear the cry of our youth. Youth activists such as Greta Thunburg are standing up and speaking out regarding climate change. Others such as Shamma bint Suhail Faris Mazrui (youth advocacy), Malala Yousafzi (women's girls education), Yari Shahidi (women & girls engagement), Mari Copeny known Little Miss Flint (water access) all those mentioned are youth who made a choice to stand up and make a difference. Malala Yousafzai says, "There is a moment when you have to choose whether to be silent or to stand up." We need more youth to stand for civility in order to create sustainable change for a better tomorrow. Who do you know that can become the change agent for civility? Perhaps the change starts with you. Each of the 4C's presents an opportunity for everyone to consider how they can be an agent of change.

The 4C's as a tool will establish conversations, and intentional conversation to solve a problem among dynamic emerging leaders. We explored various topics and trends that influence us nationally and globally. When I was growing up in the early 80's we were taught that children were to be seen and not heard.

As a parent, World Civility Ambassador and Youth Civility Activist I no longer subscribe to this notion. I have learned so much from the young girls we mentor with Blessed Girl. Young people catch things that adults may overlook. When we are looking for solutions let's include our young adults. Let's ask questions and tap into their minds for answers. I learn so much when I listen to young people. They have an insatiable appetite for solutions, technology, diversity and inclusiveness. Jesus valued the children. In The Bible Mark 10:14 "Let the children come to me, for such is the kingdom of God." Jesus was open to love & listen to children. Listening demonstrates love.

Adults are busy "adulting" and preoccupied with their own concerns and stressors to listen and consider the concerns of the youth. Our children's concerns, anxieties and challenges often are not addressed and supported. This book shares stories, experiences, insights, and topics for you to listen, learn, and live civility.

Sustainable change is the beginning of sustainable development. You can change something today and go back to the old way tomorrow. We can talk about change. We can complain about the way things currently are. We can cry and pray over our current circumstances. For a better tomorrow we must create sustainable change. We all agree that change is necessary in various areas of our lives. We may need to make changes in our community, organizations and governments and perhaps our personal relationship.

We all can agree that we do not want things to get worse than they are today. We should make an attempt to make things better. This requires forward intentional action. In 2015 Psychology Today.com informed us that 1 of 5 key elements to sustainable change is self-confidence. Self confidence in my opinion is a critical element for youth civility. Our youth need confidence. I consider confidence nothing more than having a strong belief in one's God-given ability to learn, create, lead and duplicate.

The Cambridge English Dictionary defines sustainability as an ability to continue over time. Youth Civility is a way to continue the changes that are created today. As adults instilling self-confidence and leadership skills in our youth is essential to maintaining positive change. As the future unfolds we have to continuously and progressively adapt to change.

As a mother to 3 young men, I have joyfully learned to allow my children to develop in their own ability, creativity and ingenuity to make decisions. Don't get me wrong. As a mother, this is one of the hardest lessons I had to learn and apply. One of the many benefits of mentoring youth is that I developed a true understanding of the power of possibility. By being open to listen and learn from others opens the door to mastering civility. A bonus to this is, it teaches our youth to value the opinions and creativity of others, especially those they are not familiar or comfortable with.

It creates a domino effect. This effect continues and ushers in true sustainable change. One's ability to listen and consider practices and services that they may not truly understand models an openness. Ultimate confidence happens when you know who you are and what you were created to create. Yes, you were created to create. "In the beginning God created the heavens and the earth" Genesis 1:1 The Bible begins with God creating.

I consider this purpose. As a Women & Youth Civility Ambassador I have traveled the world and met many young people along the way. One of my gifts is to help young people not only consider their purpose but to grow into it with The 4C's. Most adults do not understand or consider their purpose. If they are lucky to understand and move in their purpose it's typically later on in life. My purpose is to help young people operate in their purpose while they are young. Identifying purpose creates and builds self-confidence. Youth leaders become adult leaders. Then they go and create other leaders, simply because they know what it looks like and how it can impact others.

The 4C's gives women and girls a platform to consider their own ideas, experiences and passions in one of the C's. We have gone even further to have them communicate and share those insights in this book.

Civility is foundational to good leadership. Civility authorizes you to consider someone else. Considering how- what you do or choose not to do, may affect someone else. This is the beginning of sustainable change. Imagine a world where each person takes into consideration how their daily actions or inactions can affect the next person. My imagination led me to this work of using the 4C's to create sustainable change. I am inviting you to use your imagination as you read each chapter and see yourself as the solution. See yourself as the answer.

A key point to civility is receptiveness to diversity of thought. Understanding diverse perspectives and ideas is the key ingredient for creating and sustaining positive change. One's ability to consider someone else's ideas, perspectives and solutions creates a successful recipe for a better tomorrow. No one person has all the answers. Collectively we can!

I enjoy traveling. By traveling I have learned how connected we are as human beings. The connection brings me to ponder my own actions and how they can cause a result or reaction for someone else. Through this book you will see the connection between civility, community, creativity and climate change. I envision it as a 3-strand braid or cord of community, creativity and climate change, wrapped or held together with civility.

The last chapters are concerning climate change where we recognize it is a global issue that certainly connects all the other C's. In order for us to minimize the effects of climate we must first recognize that it is real. Climate change is recognizable. Climate change is happening all around us. Climate change is altering our landscape. It is time to ring the alarm and respond before it's too late. Climate change is as if you live in a house:

the roof is on fire and the basement is flooding. The water is rising and the ceiling is caving in and some of us are sitting comfortably as if nothing is happening. We are sounding the alarm and providing a road map to get out of our current circumstances and create sustainable change for a better tomorrow.

I recall the first time I heard about global warming. It was the former Vice President of the United States Mr. Al Gore. Al Gore was an environmentalist He served with President Bill Clinton and ran for President against George W. Bush and lost in a close race. Mr. Gore was the first leader I remember who spoke about the planet, shined a light   on the topic and made information on global warming available on the internet.

In 2007 he won a shared Nobel Peace Prize "for their efforts to build up and disseminate greater knowledge about man-made climate change, and to lay the foundations for the measures that are needed to counteract such change.", according to TheNobelPeacePrize.com

Here we are 15 years later and not much has been done to counteract climate change, and some people still don't recognize it as a true issue or consideration. Engaging our youth and women is essential for climate change because women and children are the most vulnerable and most likely to feel the effects of it.

Our authors share the insights and inspirations regarding civility. Civility always considers connection and communication as the guide and formula to success.

> *"Children must be taught how to think not what to think"* *Margaret Mead*

I have invited these authors to share what they think about The 4C's and what they think you can do to help create sustainable change.

I now encourage you to be open to the possibilities of understanding a new way, a different way to get to a desired position. Each writer shares their ideas on how they learned and developed so far.

The perspectives of our youth and women should be valued and celebrated. My research and experience taught me when youth are equipped and developed as leaders most of them will keep going and growing as leaders. Girls and women are the most likely to serve in their community and once educated even if they travel abroad they are more likely to return to their homeland and give back to their community. Unfortunately, they are the least likely to be given access to education and economic empowerment. Those that will make a difference are the last we consider for giving a chance at leadership. This must change. I am changing that with BlessedGirls Global and our 4C Curriculum. In order to have sustainable change we must have equal participation in the process. My passion and purpose is to spark the brain that will change the world.

Youth need to be taught how to lead. Youth will lead once they are allowed. Once you train, equip and educate youth they can do incredible things. Often adults consider youth especially troubled youth or disadvantaged youth as the problem. I want to change that narrative and provide a way for young people to see themselves as a solution to the problems in their own community and abroad. We need our young people to be empowered with possibility and tap into their creativity and make change happen. "Let us not discount our young people but rather let us invest and believe in them." Dr. Anana Phifer-Derilhomme

Key ingredient for community is unity. Coming together with a community brings unity. Community breeds togetherness. The power begins when people unite. Youth civility leaders appreciate and value the generations before them. These leaders see the value in shared wisdom of experience.

There's a high demand for creative people. Creative people are needed. They are in demand. Most social media platforms feature and pay people to create and share their creations.

Most education systems do not nurture creative people. Our current systems tend to instill uniformity and stifles the creatives. Artists always stand outside of the box.

Get comfortable, make time to read and enjoy the chapters coming in The 4C's!

Dr. Anana Phifer-Derilhomme
570-656-2550
apdfavored@gmail.com
www.blessedgirls.com
www.ananaphifer.com

Dr. Phifer-Derilhomme is an Entrepreneur, Author, Speaker, Success Coach and Mentor to girls and women around the world. She is a Regional Statesmen of IChange Nations. Dr. Anana Phifer-Derilhomme is the President & Founder of BlessedGirls, a Non-Profit Youth Leadership and Mentor Organization with a resourceful curriculum that educates girls and highlights female leaders from around the world to empower youth to be the change agents needed in their community to end poverty and stand for equality. 2022 BlessedGirls hosted the first 4C Youth Civility Global Tour in Burundi, Kenya, Ghana & South Africa.

Dr. Phifer-Derilhomme was awarded the 2022 Black Girlz Rock Pressure Award and recognized for blazing a trail and dominating globally in youth civility. She is the recipient of The

2020 World Greatness Award in London, UK. As an International World Civility Ambassador, Dr. Anana Phifer-Derilhomme uses her wisdom and ability to direct important public issues regarding humanity and work with girls and women globally. She is the creator of the BlessedGirl Superhero - BGS (black teenage girl superhero). BGS is a cartoon character that educates, inspires and encourages girls to develop a positive self-image, business development, and community leadership.

Dr. Phifer-Derilhomme is the Founder, Coach and Trainer with Moms on A Mission. MOMS Organization trains women to transform their lives with on-line program "Mission I-AM Possible", where women heal, grow, rejuvenate and stimulate their passion and fulfill their God-given purpose. The program provides proven success strategies that help others acknowledge, develop and fulfill their greatness. She is privileged to work with a team of inspiring business partners in the United States, London, Canada, South America and USVI. She is a Certified John Maxwell Coach and Trainer with proven success strategies to help you design and develop the life you dream of. As a business and confidence coach she can help you get to your next BIG WIN by getting clear, confident and courageous about your purpose & destiny.

Anana is a four-time author (The 4C's Creating Change For A Better Tomorrow Starts Today, A Mother's Love: Letters to Our Sons, Live Your Best Life: Answer the Call & BlessedGirl Superhero: Book of Affirmations)

She is a dedicated wife and mother to 3 extraordinary young men. Dr. Phifer-Derilhomme is simply a blessed girl- blessed with the ability to help others discover, appreciate and manifest their blessings. She is sought-out for being an enthusiastic and accountable leader. As a professional speaker, mentored by

Professor Dr. Ruben West-Black Belt Speakers Global & Prof Ambassador Dr Clyde Rivers, she speaks at conferences, churches, and community events about the importance of personal development, entrepreneurship, community, and self-empowerment. Anana has the gift and calling to get you to see past your fears & limitations, overcome your obstacles, no longer settle but SOAR into Greatness!

> *"As the butterfly evolves, so do we as God's chosen vessels to live a life of passion & purpose." Anana*

Civility:
THE ROAD-MAP TO RESPECT; LOVE; AND COURAGE

Tamika Thomas

> *"It is not our difference that divides us. It is our inability to recognize, accept, and celebrate those differences." Andre Lorde*

Civility is a powerful word. It can change social norms with powerful movements. It's a word that demonstrates a way of living and behaving, it inspires individuals to socially behave with characteristics of respect, building healthy friendships or relationships, and awareness of "self" especially how we represent ourselves by curtailing our own immediate self-interest when appropriate. Maya Angelou described Civility using these words, "In all my work, what I try to say is that as Human Beings we are more alike than we are unalike." I believe what Maya is referencing is that we are ALL "humans" on this earth, we are designed and made the same. We all have white bones, our blood is red, and we are initially born with the same number of teeth, toes, fingers, and body parts. So, if we all bleed red and have the same genetic makeup then we must be connected somehow in some way. We can't be that unalike from each other, if underneath the outer layer, we have hearts and blood alike.

In the book of Genesis, chapter 1:26-27 scripture reads, "Then God said, let us make human beings in our image, to be like us.' (27) 'So, God created human beings in his image. In the image of God, he created them; male and female he created them." We see from the very beginning God created humanity. He created us in his image, "alike" he created humans to have community, connection, and communication with each other and Him. However, when we view the word image in the "natural" culture we believe it means perception or a lifestyle. From a world perspective, we see people often refer to "protecting" the image of their brand. A lifestyle for living that encompasses "self." But when we view the word image in the "spiritual" we're describing who God is. Uniquely, human beings correlate to God that mirrors His character and nature. Being created in God's image gives us the assurance to have dignity. It displays that God has trusted humans with the gift to love and obey him. This image of God is what we are to live according to as humans. It is the most basic, original calling. To live in his image-the light of who He is and who we should be.

If we were created in God's image, how have we become a world deficit in civility? We have let the difference in our skin color, religious affiliation, political views, choice of music, education, and social-economic status highlight our differences causing division and separation. We have become a "Me vs You" society conditioned and hungry for "Self-ism". A society is quick to judge, criticize, gossip, hate each other, show envy, abuse, and commit violent acts, as learned social behaviors. An incivility society; the opposite of civility. We are to be a world full of understanding, kindness, and respect, a society that recognizes, accepts, and celebrates our differences. A world striving for ways to connect instead of disconnecting, a world of unity instead of division. Martin Luther King Jr. said it best, "The time is always right to do what is right." Now more than ever is the time to do what is right, allow civility to lead and guide us. Time to let civility be a roadmap for "Change" a map for practicing civility, especially in the face of opposition. A powerful tool that accepts and connects us to treat each other which is something that we all want and need.

When we look at a Roadmap it is a strategic plan that defines a goal or desired outcome that includes steps or milestones needed to reach it. More importantly, a Roadmap is a directional guide that helps people find specific routes for a destination spot(s). Civility is a Roadmap for a better healthier way of living. In the book, "Choosing Civility", P.M. Forni wrote, "A crucial measure of our success in life is the way we treat one another every day of our lives. When we lesson the burden of living for those around us, we are doing well; when we add to the misery of the world we are not." Time for Civility to be a Catalyst for Change.... a Roadmap for a better tomorrow.

The Roadmap

First, Respect!

"Respect"- the late great gospel singer Aretha Franklin said in her song, "R-E-S-P-E-C-T" find out what it means to me." In our natural eyes respect has become a taboo word. It lacks meaning and depth of human decency. As a child, my grandmother would often say, "don't disrespect your elders." I never fully understood the context of that statement until I understood other people's interpretation of Respect. For my family and many families like mine we had the belief that "children" should honor their parents, was a given. Respect was a tenet of my family's culture, even religion. If we look at it from a biblical lens, Deuteronomy 5:16 instructs, *"Honor your father and your mother, as the Lord your God commanded you, that your days may be long, and that it may go well with you in the land that the Lord your God is giving you."* To me, this scripture represents a clear foundation that should be the norm for human beings. This implies total obedience to respectfully listening to each other's differences and beliefs, without judgment or shame. More importantly, when I was younger, I viewed Respect to be something you earned and not given. This was the way society taught me especially when it came to my interpersonal skills and interactions with others who didn't share my beliefs, political views, or skin-color. However, this is different from my grandmother's view of Respect, it was something given respectfully. So how have we gotten away from learning and understanding what Respect means to others and culturally.

When we reflect on today's generation, we see there is a lack of respect among many. We have become conditioned to the word "Disrespect". For example, today's younger generation do not respect their parents, grandparents, authority figures, teachers, elders in the church, and each other. We witness this day after day through outlets like social media, school bullying, parents, youth violence, interactions with youth, and it appears that the problem continues to grow. As we take a deeper look, society has taught us it's ok to "disrespect" each other and to not respect our cultural differences, beliefs, or opinions, which has somehow normalized these misconceptions while justifying crappy behavior.

So how do we cultivate an acceptable, loving, understanding, respectable culture, we begin by looking in the mirror at ourselves to see how our belief system about respect has contributed to the damaging messaging we see today. Second, we start to have open conversations about culture differences, beliefs, and political views, and we create spaces where individuals could be heard and safe to agree to disagree without damaging consequences or negative outcomes. Lastly, we begin to allow the Holy Spirit to guide us to be a more compassionate culture so we can start to see people in the spirit and not in the flesh.

Second Road-Map strategy is Love.

In the book of John 3:16, "For God so loved the world, that he gave his only begotten Son, that whosoever believeth in him should not perish, but have everlasting life." Now if God could love us so much that he gave his only son, how is it that we cannot do the same. Are we willing to sacrifice ourselves and die to the flesh to follow God's instructions? How difficult is it to love each other like God continues to love us? In the book of James 2:8-9, "Yes indeed, it is good when you obey the royal law as found in the scriptures: Love your neighbor as yourself. But if you favor some people over others, you are committing a sin. You are guilty of breaking the law." This is a simple command given from God but, we as human beings made in his image has yet to achieve. Simply Put: it is time to start showing kindness, unconditional love, and respect to each other as instructed by God. Start by simply leaning into others who appear to be different from you; speak and say hello, practice acts of kindness, give without receiving, love without limitations, seek to understand instead of judging, and learn to speak the truth with love instead of finding faults, but most importantly, learn to forgive. 1 Peter 4:8, "Most important of all, continue to show deep love for each other, for love covers a multitude of sins." Let's LOVE on each other more. It's a simple act; but it starts with YOU!

Third Road-Map Strategy is Courage!

The Oxford dictionary defines Courage as: "the ability to do something that frightens one." Let's have the courage to change and dismantle a damaging practice that has served no righteous purpose in the world or society. Let's be BOLD to stand for what is right in the face of incivility and knock down oppressive systems that continue to divide instead of uniting. Let's walk together and be courageous as there are benefits when we are courageous when it's time to stand up and speak; and also, when we learn how to sit down and listen. Courage is a human activity that teaches us how to grow & learn, help others, say sorry when wrong, practice gratitude, and responsibility and accountability, but most importantly, courage is Love. And in return when we act courageously it generally makes us feel better, because it involves putting our differences aside to gain a greater outcome. So, take the steps to be Courageous for Change.

> *I will leave you with this quote by Mary Wortley Montagu," CIVILITY COSTS NOTHING AND BUYS EVERYTHING."*

TAMIKA THOMAS

Tamika Thomas, is a Licensed Professional Counselor (LPC), the owner of Urban Collective Counseling, LLC (a mental health practice), in Denver, Colorado and a National Certified Counselor (NCC). Tamika is a certified yoga teacher and obtained her 200-hour teacher training certificate from Satya Yoga Cooperative. The only BIPOC yoga teacher training in the Nation. In addition, she completed a 200-hour Grieving Mindful teacher training with the Grief Support Network.

Prior to becoming a Mental Health Clinician, she worked as a youth case manager working with high risk youth and their families in diverse settings. She has extensive experience working with women and young adults. Tamika enjoys utilizing an integrative approach in her therapy practice, primarily using a Person-Centered, Mindfulness, and Cognitive-Behavioral Therapy approach. She is passionate about breaking the stigma surrounding mental health and taking a passenger-seat approach to the therapy process. Having worked in underserved communities for years, she enjoys helping clients with adjusting to their current stage of life.

Tamika is dedicated to her community and has volunteered and served on various boards and community organizations through-out Colorado. She is committed to bringing Change and welcomes the opportunity to work with the unique issues that many POC youth and their families face.

Moreover, Tamika is the mother to 4 sons' and loves spending time with her children, family and friends. She enjoys cooking, trying new foods, laughing, and being a daughter of Christ.

COMPLEXITY OF CIVILITY

Nasset Derilhomme

Civility, as per the Merriam-Webster dictionary, can be defined as "civilized conduct," or "a polite act or expression". Though this provides a basic framework for the term, I would argue that it falls short of encapsulating its true significance. Despite the alluring comfort that may come with sharing my experiences and reaching some grand conclusion about our moral obligation to uphold civil standards, I feel that doing so would be to undermine the complexity of the term, and specifically its implications when applied to our behavior. Ultimately, civility--just as any other moniker of human activity--is far too intricate to be defined in simple terms, and the mere attempt to do so minimizes the role that civility plays in our world, specifically as we become interconnected in an age that has seen an exponential growth of globalization. More so than at any other time in our history, we are exposed to cultures and ways of life from different parts of the world. We must accompany this transition with a heightened awareness to ideas which contradict our own, as an understanding of them will be vital in facilitating relationships between different groups.

In examining the current state of world affairs, it often seems that we have lost sight of what connects us beyond our political affiliation, religious observances, or cultural practices. Beneath all of these veils of disguise lies the bare face of an individual capable of complex emotions and susceptible to the changes around them. Only at the point at which we all come to see ourselves in one another will we ever see a meaningful shift in the ways in which we deal with each other, and only then will civility be a guiding principle in our conduct.

One person whose work I would like to highlight is James Baldwin, who was an author and activist most prevalent during the American Civil Rights Movement in the mid-20th century. Similar to many other prominent figures throughout this period, his work focuses on the relationship that exists between African Americans and their white counterparts, though he takes on a perspective distinct from many others by extending the burden of alleviating the tensions between the two unto the white population specifically. Other notable figures of the time, such as Martin Luther King and Malcolm X, made calls for action and declarations of what must be done for the advancement of African Americans in society. Baldwin, on the other hand, placed a greater emphasis on the psyche of American society and the realizations that we must come to as a collective to bring about change. Through his exploration of the Black experience, he notes his perception of white Americans as one filled less with anger and more of a recognition of their own downfalls which they, themselves, fail to realize. This, however, is not to minimize the former, as such sentiments may be justified given the circumstances. Rather (through my own interpretation), he defines how their position *minimizes* their ability to uphold true standards of civility because, for so long, white Americans have been able to view themselves as the pinnacle of world society. Since its conception, the United States has been one of, if not the most influential player on the world stage. Its influence stretches beyond borders, and this seamless leverage has only been made more prevalent with our transition into the digital age.

Looking at history, even outside of the United States, it is difficult to find a time in which white people (I use the term loosely) had not used some form of persuasion to delude the world, themselves included, into believing that their standards of living are somehow more viable than those of others. Take, for example, the use of the term "the white man's burden". Coined by English journalist Rudyard Kipling, the term is defined as "a duty formerly asserted by white people to manage the affairs of nonwhite people whom they believed to be less developed." In order to justify their widespread expansion into outside territories, American imperialists used this idea to emphasize the necessity that they spread their beliefs of Christianity, their practice of democracy, and their standards of development unto people who abided by a culture that was deemed to be inferior.

I would also like to be very clear that, although the United States is the case which I have chosen to highlight, it is far from the only instance in which the phenomenon of our perception has misled our ability to view the world objectively. On the global scale, there has been a repeated cycle of the notion of indoctrinated superiority.

A major event in our current state of affairs is the conflict between Russia and its border nation of Ukraine. With an invasion launched on February 24, 2022, the Russian President Vladimir Putin claims that the goal was to "demilitarize and de-Nazify" Ukraine, though it is largely believed that the attack is based more so disassociating Ukraine from the western defense alliance, NATO. Regardless of the reasoning, the conflict has caused widespread condemnation of the Russian government and has prompted and international response to aid Ukraine in its defense through actions such as military support and significant sanctions to weaken the Russian economy. This, in itself, serves as an example of what can be done when international forces cooperate to halt what has been deemed to be a violation of human rights and state sovereignty. However, it becomes more telling in the scope of civility when it is compared to the response to other instances of such violations in different parts of the world. Perhaps the most persist example of this is Middle East, a region consistently plagued with conflict due, in part, to religious strife and involvement from the Western World. Following the invasion of Ukraine, a reporter for CBS, a popular American television network, was quoted saying that "... this isn't a place, with all due respect, like Iraq or Afghanistan, that has seen conflict raging for decades... this is a relatively civilized, relatively European--I have to choose those words carefully, too--city where you wouldn't expect that or hope that it's going to happen," (Business Insider). Another reporter from the French-based news channel BFM TV said that "We're not talking about Syrians fleeing the bombing of the Syrian regime backed by Putin; we're talking about Europeans leaving in cars that look like ours to save their lives," (Los Angeles Times). Although apologies followed these statements on both occasions, the inherent attitude is one that cannot be overlooked. It has become a severely commonplace tradition across the Western World of limiting our empathic sentiments to those who look like us; I use "us" in a way that transcends physical appearance--though this is undeniably significant--to also imply the importance of similar political theories, religious affiliations, and overall cultural resemblance. This reaction from the media uncovers an intuitive belief that our systems are superior, and consequently, others must rise to our level of civility in order to be recognized, and thus treated, as equal--a harsh impediment to the goal of civility.

This, then, is what I propose has made the notion of civility seem so hard to come by. For so long, we have accepted standards of civility as synonyms for assimilation, and we determine who merits our civil treatment based on their alignment with our own values. Though this may seem to be a natural occurrence, it becomes a very dangerous one when our value system is directly linked to who we view as similar to ourselves, and a certain tribal mentality arises which antagonizes any opposition.

The question that arises, then, is: how is civility instilled into the world around us? Unfortunately, however, there is no simple answer, and the proof of this lies in the list of historical figures that we praise for their efforts in condemning disparate treatment of different groups of people. Though their work pushes for substantial change and, at times, succeeds in doing so, we continue to see significant discrepancies in the treatment of people based on natural characteristics.

As it was noted at the beginning of this chapter, humans are complex beings, and problems associated with dealing with collective groups are ones which offer no straightforward solution. This, I know, sets up a somewhat bleak outlook on the world, but it is not to say that a solution does not exist.

I believe that the most pivotal part in progressing towards true civility is a willingness to acknowledge when you are wrong. We often become so engulfed in our own perspective that the only term of any agreement is discrediting the merit of any opposing viewpoint. Rather than challenging our opinions, we attempt to validate them by surrounding ourselves with others who think likewise. Rather, we must set aside our inclination to view ourselves as contestants to one another and realize that it is through an understanding of each other that we can ultimately better conditions for us all.

I spoke extensively before about James Baldwin and his appearing refusal to view white Americans as a collective evil for their wrongdoings in the past. In my favorite Baldwin piece, *The Fire Next Time*, he states that "It is so simply a fact and one that is so hard, apparently, to grasp: *Whoever debases others is debasing himself.* That is not a mystical statement but a most realistic one, which is proved by the eyes of any Alabama sheriff--and I would not like to see Negroes ever arrive at so wretched a condition." A condition. Baldwin encapsulates an entire history of malpractice and diagnoses it just as a doctor would an illness, and I believe that this is a very telling element of how we must view one another when striving towards a world which truly upholds civility. I would also like to extend this point by adding that this "condition" is one that we all suffer from. As I see it, what spurs the illness is no more than the fact that, for so long, white Americans have engulfed themselves in a reality which they have created for themselves, and a society in which they have been lucky enough to come to view themselves as the pinnacle. Although circumstances change, the natural phenomenon of people becoming so immersed in an echo chamber of reinforcements of their own belief is one that applies to everyone. Thus, we all enter situations with our own bias that may alter our ability to see things objectively. With this understanding, if we truly desire to promote this ideal of civility, we must enter all situations with an open mind and a willingness to accept that our own prejudices exist and concede that we may be in the wrong. Even further than this, we can seek to understand the impact that our thoughts, both individually and collectively, have had on others.

Although optimistic, I must not be naive enough to hope that the words I have written will change the world, even in a marginal sense. The world is too intricate; as are we, the people who inhabit it. I previously mentioned the long list of historical figures who we praise for their contributions in advancing us towards civility, yet the current state of things may suggest that, even with their efforts, this fable of civility is just that--an unattainable fallacy which we cling onto for the mechanism of hope. Though this is a compelling narrative, it is one that I refuse to accept. Perhaps I am yet to lose my innocence. Perhaps

I am yet to come to terms with the fact that all things borne will be borne again, and thus the way things have been the way that they will persist to be. In either case, I believe that the stride toward true civility is one worth taking, and that to succumb to this assumption that it is effectively futile is to abandon the work that has already been done.

What must accompany this is a great deal of patience. Reasonably so, frustration is a commonplace reaction to dealing with many of the world's evils. Although any form of prejudice is an antonym to civility, it must be understood that it is synonymous with reality, and when working to resolve them, you are simultaneously working to uncover the various frames that shape an individual's reality. For this reason, it is vital that we facilitate discussion between groups of distinct perspectives, as these conversations create an environment in which thoughts can be shared and if the gap between our differences cannot be bridged, a marginal understanding can be obtained of an opinion foreign to our own. It must be stressed, however, that any substantial change will not be made overnight and that all of us, in taking part in such an initiative, are bearers of the belief in "creating change today to create a better tomorrow". Change that will take time to manifest and a tomorrow which we may not live to see.

Nasset Derilhomme is a sophomore student at Northeastern University with a major in International Business & International Affairs with a minor in Law and Public Policy. Throughout Middle and High School, Nasset was a member of the Perth Amboy Chapter of New Jersey Orators, a non-profit organization that teaches public speaking, civic engagement, and an appreciation for literature in preparation for advanced learning. At several state competitions, he was recognized for outstanding performance. In high school, he spearheaded an initiative to create a Black Student Union, with the goal of fostering a safe place for students of color while sharing the experience of Black students amongst others. He also served as the first President of the club, creating a framework for the club to effectively operate in the years to come. In addition, he was a member of the Future Business Leaders of America, in which he worked both individually and collaboratively to understand and apply fundamental business principles to improve on technical problem-solving skills. Nasset is an ambitious, detail-oriented individual with a desire to use a professional platform to address issues involving social and economic inequity on a global scale. He carries an eagerness to grow through collaboration, while also being willing and able to take on leadership positions.

Phone: 732-672-6821
Email: nasset11@gmail.com
Instagram: its_nasset
LinkedIn: Nasset Derilhomme

COMMUNITY

Community creates opportunity for collaboration, consideration and elevation. It takes a community to elevate a group of people. Community is built on beliefs, belonging and brother/ sisterhood. Ubuntu-I am because you are. In a community we understand and appreciate the need and reliance on each other.

THE MORE YOU ARE *INVOLVED* THE MORE YOU *EVOLVE*

Ayanna Slacum

What does a community look like? Who are usually involved in the community? What does your community offer? Is your community safe? How many communities do you belong to? These are the questions that come to mind when I think of a community.

Communities represent people coming together to solve differences and communicating to provide useful and meaningful resources for their people. Community also includes allowing people to nurture and create opportunities and experiences. In a community, the most important thing is making sure that everyone feels included as well as appreciated. Community has impacted me because I feel like the more you are *involved* the more you *evolve*.

I have evolved in my community by helping plan county-wide events that create safe space to connect with others and gain resources or positive experiences. I volunteer at the events to help coordinate activities, recruit other youth volunteers and assist in any way that I can. I evolved as an individual by being able to act in a professional setting as well as trying to be more accepting and understanding of information and situations. This means thinking and really trying to understand what I am being asked rather than responding first. Also trying to make sure that I ask questions and stay engaged while being with others. My mentors Tracey, Sarah, Sean, and Lindsey have impacted my involvement. I say Sean because he introduced me to these amazing women. The ladies have impacted me by giving me the opportunity to be their intern and be able to help them whenever and wherever they need. Community connects people and different opportunities that exposes you to extraordinary experiences to enhance your scope. It helps you form new connections and relationships. This is really important because you never know how you can be impacted and or inspired to do something.

Community has a huge impact on me, growing up I was always involved in *something*. As a little girl, I was an active member of my church, I sang in the choir and I danced (an expressive and spiritual dancing to Gospel music). I also participated in afterschool programs, extra-curricular activities including Rutgers University Upward Bound (a program for first generation and low-income students to have the opportunity to be exposed to a pre-college program). Upward Bound was significant because the program exposed me to resources like College visits, SAT-test taking courses, Broadway theater shows, Summer institution and so much more), and volunteering at Saint Peters Hospital. During that experience, I transported patients, made take-home packets, answered the phone in the office, delivered orders to different departments, and lastly filed paperwork, and so much more. All these diverse and amazing experiences helped shape me into the human being that I am today.

I love to give back and see a smile on someone's face because I helped *them*. For example, I help out with an organization called Sister Work Excel it is a mentorship program that engages the youngest of the Latin community by hosting monthly events covering workshops on mentorship, leadership, financial literacy, prevention of sexual violence. Here I have the opportunity to have monthly check in calls with the girls to make sure they are doing well, mentally, socially, and academically. I had an interaction with one girl who was stressed because of working and being a first year first generation college student. I then suggested some tips to help her out like finding a tutor, cutting down work hours and suggested coming up with a schedule. Then at our next check in she told me she was doing so much better and incorporated some of my suggestions to help her out. When I heard that it made me so excited and proud to know that I was able to help her and she actually listened and is doing better. Helping people is one of my favorite things to do. For example, in 2020 my hometown community (New Brunswick, New Jersey) held a Juneteenth celebration sponsored by the local NAACP chapter. The different NAACP chapters came together to teach and engage people around the city of New Brunswick and surrounding cities, on the historic evolution of Juneteenth especially since this was the first year that Juneteenth was recognized as a state and federal holiday. The national holiday celebrates ALL slaves being finally free. My church's praise team and I danced, and to see the look on people's faces in the crowd, it shocked me. There were so many expressions and different races but to see everyone at the end really made me happy. The types of expressions were as if they felt God's presence or if they felt the moves that we were doing with a mix of the words to the song. This is because they were praising us for how we did but also were impacted by the song "War Cry" by Queen Naija. We chose this song because we felt like it went really well with the theme of the event. It has helped me to be open to try new and different things. In the song Queen says, "Oh and I say devil you can't have my mind, devil you can't have my soul, I belong to God and I'm fighting you off, With the power of the Holy Ghost". This is powerful because it just expresses how we as Christians and or people in general should not let negative things (such as the devil) get to you and affect the way that you act towards people and yourself.

A scripture that connects is "Joseph replied, "Don't be afraid. Do I act for God? Don't you see, you planned evil against me but God used those same plans for my good, as you see all around you right now—life for many people. Easy now, you have nothing to fear; I'll take care of you and your children." He reassured them, speaking with them heart-to-heart."(MSG Genesis 50:19-21).This is stating what the devil meant for evil, God means for good. This demonstrates that you know who you believe in as far as a high power (God) and you know who will be there for you in times of struggle and need. I really just loved this song and thought that it was good because this was the first event since the COVID-19 shutdown. It has also helped me to be less afraid of meeting new people and forming new relationships. It has also helped me gain skills that I will need to use in settings I am not normally in.

Being in and a part of the community has really helped me overcome some challenges. I grew up in New Brunswick, NJ off of Exit 9 on the New Jersey turnpike. New Brunswick is one of the cities in Middlesex County, New Jersey. This city hosts the county seat of Middlesex County and is the home of Rutgers University. Not only is it a regional commercial hub for the Central New Jersey region, but it's also a growing and major commuter town for residents commuting to New York City. New Brunswick City has a population of 55,266, which registers an increase of 88 people from the 55,181 persons at the 2010 United States census enumeration. Further, the Census Bureau's Population Estimate program ranked New Brunswick City as the 689th most populous city in 2019. New Brunswick City hosts production facilities and corporate headquarters for several pharmaceutical companies, such as Bristol Myers Squibb and Johnson and Johnson pharmaceuticals. In addition, this city is famous due to its ethnic diversity. It hosts different communities all over, which brings gentrification to the town(from city website). Some challenges that I faced was not wanting to be outside due to gun violence. I say this because growing up my mom, Taneesha Slacum, always said you have to be careful because "bullets have no names on them". Hearing this scared me and watching the News I always saw someone getting stabbed and or shot. I was scared that this could happen to someone in my neighborhood or even worse, my family or friends. I feel like it really gave me anxiety towards any type of violence or conflict. I don't like shows or movies that have killing or any type of violence. I also did not really want to be outside because it felt like there was nothing positive to do. I suffered from boredom, and I was not engaged in my community. I did not connect with the people near my home. Most of the people I was friends with did not live nearby, I was too young to walk, or my mom was too busy to take me. This made me feel lonely and isolated from the world.

This is something that tends to happen often to people growing up and increases young people's desire to connect to something and want to "fit in" with their peers. In order to grow out of this, you have to get involved and try to meet people and make friends so that you can have a better experience in your community. You can try new things to see if you like them and that will help you when you explore the world and yourself. One of the organizations that has been present in my life growing up is the Civic League of Greater New Brunswick. The Civic League is a non-profit community-based organization operated to strengthen African American families and other minority family groups. This is accomplished by advocating, promoting, and providing community-based services that empower families and improve their quality of life. While being in this program I participated in the after-school program in 5th grade, extended school day program in middle school, 7th grade step up and 8th grade leadership, and I was in Ladies of Vision from middle school all the way up until I graduated high school. 5th - 10-11 years old, 6th grade 11-12 yrs old, 7th grade - 12-13 yrs old, high school - 14-18 yrs old. Being an active member of this organization, I had the opportunity to meet this man named Mr. Sean Hewitt when I was 10 years old and we have maintained a strong relationship since then. He has been the best father figure and mentor I could have ever asked for. I say this because he has really been here every step of the way to see me grow and blossom. I am just so grateful and honored to have him in my life. A time where he showed up for me was when my older brother went to jail. He was not only there for myself, but he was there for my family as well and this meant a lot because he helped mentor my older brother. This was also really important because it was just my mom and all of us trying to figure everything out and this was new to us and we did not know what to do and or how things would go. So having someone I can talk to about my feelings and frustration, help me to cope and understand, pointing me to resources inside my school, and also putting me in programs so that I can be able to try and get my mind off the situation. I know that when I am stressed, angry, or just need someone to let me vent I can go to him, and he will listen and then ask me if he can give advice.

Advisement from mentors is so important because they are people who guide you and make you feel confident. It is more likely for us to listen to them because they are not our parents and as children, we tend to think our parents do not know what they are talking about. With mentors they are important to have and go to when you need advice because they can help you with things that your parents may not know the answers to and or be someone else that plays a huge role in your support system. He showed me a lot of things that I did not know growing up and he also introduced me to many people I did not know from the community. Some things that he and the program taught me was how to set up a table properly, leadership skills, stepping out of your comfort zone, and making the best of any situation.

One year with the Ladies of Vision program we went to Frost Valley YMCA. Frost Valley is 3 hours away from my home in New Brunswick, located in Claryville, New York, in the valley of the Catskill Mountains. We stayed overnight there for 3 days and 2 nights. I was so nervous to leave because we were going in the middle of nowhere and had no phone service. I did not know what to expect or what we were going to do. I am a picky eater as well, so I did not know what we were going to eat either. While being there we walked on a cable bridge over water, climbed a rock wall, climbed wooden bars that kind of look like Jenga blocks and so many more things that I had never done before. It was a new adventure. We slept in cabins, played games at night, made smores and so much more bonding activities. After this amazing trip I wanted to go again. It was such an amazing experience that helped me figure out what I do not like, what I will and will not do when it comes to stepping out of my comfort zone. Lastly, it was just such an amazing learning experience.

During February Mr. Hewitt called me and said, "Hey honey would you like to read to kids" I said "Yes, of course when and where?" he then stated "it will be virtual and you will have a call before for introductions" I said "Okay no problem just let me know". There I had the opportunity to meet Sarah, Tracey, and Lindsey. I was so nervous because I did not know who they were or how their vibe was going to be. It is important for you to do things that you feel nervous about because that shows you to yourself that you are growing as an individual and you are stepping out of your comfort zone. This is also important because you do not know what opportunities and or how your relationship and networking will be if you do not go and step out of your comfort zone. Then I went in with an open mind and it was so amazing. They were so nice, funny, and so wise. Being able to interact with people virtually after not having any interaction was amazing and to still feel the connection was even better. After meeting them this first time I kept on coming back to work with them and then they started mentoring me. Being with my mentors is opening doors that have never been open before.

Over my Spring Break I went back home, and I was working with my mentors at their office. When I go there, I sit in meetings, sometimes I visit different places to consider hosting community events, as well as researching some places in an area where we can invite more people to our events. It is important to get more people out to events because letting them know that they have these events and activities in their community that includes art, history, culture and or curiosity about these particular categories. They are also giving us the opportunity to let us know what they want when they come to the events as well as what they would like to see and take part in. The Arts Institute of Middlesex County had a really big meeting this particular time when I included all the people that they work with as well as the administrators. This was really big for me because I was the youngest person in the room full of people in seats that I will someday be sitting in myself. Also, I am probably the only person at my age that is doing this. It pushes me to keep going and make sure that I graduate college so that I can be the head boss at a meeting someday.

During the meeting I was put on the spot to introduce myself to the team and I also shared that I was writing my chapter for this book that I am currently writing as I prepare to travel to Africa. After the meeting Nancy, a consultant for the organization who had traveled across the country to participate in this meeting came up to me and stated, "Oh my you are so professional when speaking and can really be an amazing and professional businesswoman". When she said this to me, I was so amazed and touched, this being because no one has ever said this to me and I never had an opportunity to be in a space to be able to do this. So, her reaction was really shocking to me. It also made me look and think to myself *like wow you are such an amazing and powerful young lady I cannot wait to see you excel and achieve all your goals and aspirations in life.* The power of positive thinking, mentorship, and how building up your self-confidence can help you make a difference in the world. This really opened my eyes to make me want to be a youth leader of my community because I see the impact of how being involved positively impacts the community members.

Being part of my community has taught me that I need to be considerate with every aspect of life and not just think about one thing but every aspect of my life. Sometimes just thinking about one thing can make you miss out on opportunities and once in a lifetime experiences. I have realized that it is important to take any resource or opportunity that comes my way because I do not know if it will come back my way and/or how it can help me to help others.

A leader in my community is my mentor, Tracey O'Reggio Clark. This woman is so phenomenal I am so grateful and appreciative of her. God knew what He was doing when he placed her in my life. I say this because she has helped me so much when it comes to reaching my goal to pay for college on scholarships. She has also been there through my college process and helped me consider some things that I did not consider when attending college. I met her in February of 2021 when I had the opportunity to kick off the Art & Storytime program as the first teen reader and our relationship continues to grow. She has been guiding me through as I am growing into being a youth community leader and making sure that I know what appropriate and professional protocols are.

Ms. Clark helped me improve my communication skills when texting, emailing, typing, and speaking. These skills prepared me for my scholarship writings and interviews. She has also pushed me to step out of my comfort zone when it comes to eating and encouraged me to explore new activities. I really appreciate and honor the things that she does for me because I feel like it takes a weight off my mom's shoulders being that these are not things that she knows or can help me with so it is good to have someone else there to help me where my mom cannot during this process.

You find other people that are familiar with the similar interests as you, it allows you to confide in them and also knowing that they are older and wiser you know that you can trust their judgements and opinions. It is important to know that you can connect and form close relationships and bonds with community members and strong mentors because they will always be a resource to you, having them there to answer questions, and also knowing that you have a strong advocate that is very mindful about strategic steps in order to achieve your future accomplishments and ultimate success. A strong community mentor will take the time to introduce you to their network, offer an internship in your particular career of interest, and connect you with a particular organization of your interest. Most importantly a strong mentor makes sure you are equipped with the proper tools to help yourself and to help the people you may interact with- Each one, teach one. I also find it to be funny because we have the same birthday, and we say and do a lot of the same things, so it is good to see an older version of me.

During the pandemic the community was really helpful. I say this because they were giving and sending out resources for us as people to make sure we stay safe and have things that we need. They were also trying the best that they could to still give us as members of the community something. As the pandemic started going on for a while, community organizations and partners like New Brunswick Cultural Center, The Arts Institute of Middlesex County, Civic League of Greater New Brunswick, and Garden of Healing began to host online activities. Art & Storytime, after school programs online, yoga, and so many more events. It was a rough time so I understand that they did the best that they could in the circumstances we as a community were facing.

During the pandemic kids were drastically impacted. Many students who were used to being in the classroom and now have little to no educational interaction. This means that they would go on the computer to play games and watch videos. Not to learn online and do schoolwork on the computer. Then you also had students just starting their school career and then they just jumped right into the online schooling system.

I recall my younger brother had a harder time adapting to this new style of learning than I did. I would say this because while the teacher is teaching he would want to watch TV, play the game, eat and just anything other than sitting down listening to the teacher. Many students also lost touch of social interaction and wanting to connect and meet new people. This was a result of being isolated from the world and the things and people that had easy access to before the pandemic. This time also caused people to be depressed because they were not able to go out and were forced to deal with all the things that people would escape from by going to school and work. After society began to reopen, my mentor and her team worked tirelessly to get back in the community and hoped to make an impact on the community. They started doing art in the park, first Friday networking events, Juneteenth celebrations, art festivals and so much more. Not only were they holding in person events there were other people doing the same thing. This created a sense of happiness and positivity because the community started to come together again.

AYANNA SLACUM

Sophmore at Albright College, New Brunswick Resident

Ayanna Slacum is a proud, life-long New Brunswick, New Jersey, USA resident and an Honors. Graduate of New Brunswick High School. She was accepted to over 20 universities across the country and decided to pursue her higher education at Albright College, located in Reading, PA.

This thriving Freshman currently has a 3.67 GPA and is excited to complete her major in Communications with a concentration in Advertising and Public Relations. Ayanna was recently recruited as an Admissions Student Ambassador, and elected Secretary of the student organization National Organization of Women (NOW) for Albright. During her semester breaks,

Ayanna is a Communications and Special Events Intern for the New Brunswick Cultural Center and the Arts Institute of Middlesex County, where she has participated in several events such as the NAACP's 2021 Juneteenth Celebration, the Arts Institute's Art & Story Time, the Art Institute's Art in the Park, REPLENISH (formerly known as MCFOODS) food drives and the New Brunswick City Center's annual Tree Lighting. Ayanna has been selected as a co-Author of the Book "4 C's", where she will be traveling to Africa to mentor young students about community service, education, and leadership this Summer. Ayanna is grateful and honored for the opportunity to be a co-author for the book the 4 Cs: Community, Civility, Creativity, and Climate change.

UMOJA

Adreonna Riggs

Umoja (Unity) : Maintaining unity as a family, community, and race of people.

That's what community means to me. Community means UNITY. Togetherness as people. Judah Smith wrote "Life is better together, so let's get better at this thing called "together". The word unity is a part of the word community. You can't have community without unity. The definition of unity: the state of being united or joined as a whole.   Ok I think you get the point that I'm trying to make is that unity is an essential part of community.

When I was young and all the way up until I reached thirteen or fourteen my family moved around alot. As I look back the instability enabled me to connect with the new communities or neighborhoods when we moved somewhere new. I didn't play outside with the kids and I didn't know anyone else in the neighborhood. There is this time I still remember playing in the neighborhood with the other neighborhood kids. We would play outside until the street lights came on. That was our indicator it was time to go home. This time we lived with my great grandmother Bonnie Pearl Chislom. I was outside playing and I cut my right hand climbing a fence. I didn't notice the cut right away. I was still playing with the other kids. Then all of a sudden, I felt something like water rolling down my hand. It wasn't water but blood. Now that I noticed the cut the senses of pain increased in that area. This was a pretty bad cut. I rushed home to get help. Once I got home my great grandmother directed me to go to the lady's house on the corner of the neighborhood block because she didn't have the supplies to fix my hand, but we knew the lady in the house on the corner would have it. We can call her Queen. She was welcoming, friendly and kind. The Queen lived a few houses down so I didn't have a far walk. As a kid I felt like she had everything at her house. The Queen even had a candy store in her house that sold our favorite snacks. The characteristics that Queen showed was my first exposure to someone outside of my family who genuinely cared for me that lived in my community. I noticed Queen supporting her own family and the neighborhood kids. The Queen showed umoja. Her actions showed me at a young age that there are other people outside of my family that care about me and they live right in my community. Seek OQP. I was listening to motivational speaker Les Brown and heard about OQP. It stands for Only Quality People. How do you know who's OQP? I would recommend a book called Relational Intelligence by Dr. Dharius Daniels. I absolutely love this book. Relational Intelligence breaks down characteristics in friends, associates, assignments and advisors so we can create better, impactful and meaningful relationships.

Dr. Dharius Daniels wrote "Just because a person has the ability doesn't mean they are authorized". This stood out to me when I was reading the book because it reminds me as I'm building relationships look at more than the person's ability, what are some characteristics they are showing. I encourage wisdom as we seek to find or build our communities. Relational Intelligence helped me to better identify what to look for in individuals.

I think that everyone has strengths and weaknesses. Being in the right community environment is an opportunity to exercise your strengths with the weaknesses that someone else may have. We're all unique. I want you to lean into your uniqueness. I want to share an exercise with you that I use to lean more into my uniqueness, I use reminders. I remind myself every day of my greatness by putting up sticky notes in a place I visit daily. My closet is where you will find yellow sticky notes that say I am enough, I am strong, I am blessed, I am worthy, I am talented, I am royalty. When we put the words 'I am' in the front of a word that describes us, and you read that phrase aloud daily we feed our consciousness. These reminders that I say everyday are also called affirmations or positive self-talk. Affirmations can be defined as positive phrases or statements that we repeat to ourselves (Positive Affirmations: Definition, Examples, and Exercises, 2022).

My aunt shared a job opportunity to be a faith walker. A faith walker with the Indianapolis Ten Point Coalition. Faith Walker engages individuals who are involved in high risk behaviors that lead to violence and encourage them to make better life choices. The organization hosts faith walks in selected neighborhoods in Indianapolis, in the USA. The mission of the Indianapolis TenPoint Coalition is to reduce violence and homicide through direct engagement, the promotion of education, and the fostering of employment opportunities. I was open because it was a change of scenery from my day job being inside of an office all day plus I saw it as an opportunity to build a relationship with my great aunt since she was already doing the work. I joined her team. My aunt's team was assigned to the crown hill neighborhood. If we had seasonal essential items to pass out to the people we would like hats, gloves, coats, and flyers with resource information on them. Before we would walk the streets we would join in a circle and pray. I have never done this before. I felt like we were out there for a bigger purpose. My experience walking in this neighborhood was different from when I would drive through. My observation and engagement with the neighbors I saw brokenness. The brokenness is in the relationships between neighbors. I saw brokenness with the raggedy streets and abandoned houses. No place for the children to play outside. I think the culture has lost what it means and feels like to be a part of a genuine community. A genuine community is where everyone knows each other and helps each other out. I think another good example of genuine community is Black Wall Street. Black Wall Street was a thriving community in Tusla, Oklahoma, USA in the early 1900s. This was a community that had bustling Black owned businesses, theaters, schools, social health, and a strong distribution of wealth among its middle and upper classes. Reports estimate the community had more than 10,000 African American residents, and most of them were thriving. Black Wall Street was the epitome of a self-sustaining community and strength. Black people supported each other, which allowed for easier access to resources, savings, housing, jobs, education, and health. Black Wall Street was just one of many thriving communities in the United States, but it also became a site that would serve as an example of the violence and hatred that grew out of greed from white financial interests (The History of Black Wall Street | OneUnited Bank, 2022).

I was a faith walker for about 2 years. A gift I have is the ability to see the potential and growth that can happen once the right people get together. My new level of exposure to that neighborhood motivated me to get more involved with the growth opportunities. I think change can start with at least one person. I shared my interest to want to help more in this community with my aunt. In 2019 I joined the Crown Hill Neighborhood Association also known as CHNA. CHNA is a group of volunteers that work hard through the action committees to positively impact the neighborhood also by working along with community partners (Crown Hill Neighborhood Association - Indianapolis, 2022). Once I joined the team and learned more about the organization I saw more people showed actions of umoja (unity). CHNA promotes a better environment, a cleaner place to live and for the children to play by organizing neighborhood clean ups, and placing trash bins in heavy traffic areas. This organization provides genuine help to people and does not take from them. When I joined the board of the association I was about 27 or 28 years old, the youngest and still is. Once I saw I was the youngest I knew it was a part of my mission to seek other young leaders like myself. A part of my mission and goal is to find other young leaders that want to give back to their community. If we don't start caring for our neighbors now then who will? The cycle of poverty, lack of food, and crime can continue if we dont start now to change for a better tomorrow for our future generations. Before change can start in the community it's important to hear from the actual residents to see what they want. I dont think it's healthy to just start intiviates in an area and you haven't received feedback from the residents.

A benefit of being on the Crown Hill neighborhood association board. I was a part of a team of people that showed umoja (unity).Through the different action committee I got the opportunity to exercise hearing from the residents on what they want and don't want in their neighborhood. I took the lead role in a project called Asset Mapping. Asset mapping is a way to assist in getting residents engaged with their neighborhood in a meaningful way; better understand who is willing to assist in addressing problems, issues, and concerns. We created a survey for the residents to complete to share their feedback. Once we get the feedback the team will review this data, fill the gaps and provide the resources. CHNA is a great example of a community of people coming together for a greater purpose for our further generations. Creating better habits now for a better life later.

NIA

Nia (Purpose): work collectively to build communities that will restore the greatness of African people.

Working together now as a team on initiatives that impact individual and family sustainability can create good habits to cycle into the future generations work ethics. Since I've been a part of the CHNA board, this community of people have inspired and motivated me to continue my assignment in this universe. Understanding your assignment is your task if you don't know already. Change doesn't happen overnight but it can start today with you and who you surround yourself with. What if I'm surrounded by negativity? I knew that question might come across your mind. If you are then you have to remove yourself. I experienced some negative environments. What helped me is youtube. I would search motivational videos and come across some very inspiring people. We can manifest the environment we desire . One way to manifest is being open to receiving the group of people you want to be around. You have to be clear and describe the characteristics you want. "If you can see it in your mind, you can have it in your hand"- author unknown.

Pray about it. Praying is just like talking to a trusted friend. The universe will respond to your request but you have to ask for it and believe. That's exactly what I did and got partnered with the right people. It takes time and patience. I believe being more aware of the kind of people you are surrounded by can help identify if you're in the right space or not. I challenge you to reevaluate your current relationships and see if you need to remove yourself so you can be ready for the right dream team to assist with the divine assignment. I used to think that I was some kind of super woman and that I could do everything by myself and that's completely wrong. I can't do it all alone and you can't either so stop trying to do everything by yourself. I like to follow the R.I.G.G. Principles as a reminder for my business and lifestyle R-Realize your value I-Invest in yourself at the level you want a return G-Go for what you want G- Get a dream team.

KUUMBA

Kuumba (Creativity): to find new, innovative ways to leave communities of African descent in more beautiful and beneficial ways than the community inherited.

My job as a placement specialist/account manager got eliminated in 2020 and decided to become a full-time entrepreneur? Being an entrepreneur was new to me but I had an idea that the work ethic is similar to working for someone else. I maintained being consistent, professional, and exceeded expectations at every position I served as.

However, I still didn't technically know how to get started as an entrepreneur. I didn't know very many people close to me that were successful entrepreneurs. I was missing how to get started to become a successful entrepreneur. I knew I could operate my own business from the previous experience I gained over the past 14 plus years in administration, management, coordinating, human resource, marketing and customer service. Guess what I wrote down in a notebook that in 2020 I would be running my own business and not working for someone. Then Marach 2020 I was laid off. Crazy right. Since I knew I had a lot to learn about entrepreneurship I was open to receive all the helpful information I needed to get started. I was able to lock in a mentor who helped me a lot at the start of my journey. Being exposed to that one mentor exposed me to a whole community of successful entrepreneurs and most of them want to help people like me become successful as entrepreneurs. Having a group of people, I can interact with that have common interests has helped me overcome challenges of not knowing how to become something I have never been. Once I was connected with the right people, the amount of resources that are available literally blew my mind. There is plenty of entrepreneur training and workshops. My goal is to continue to share resources that are available to everyone and make the information accessible for everyone. Even if the person doesn't use the resource you can't say it wasn't available.

IMANI

> *Imani (Faith):* the belief in God, family, heritage, leaders, and others that will lead to the victory of Africans around the world.

I believe it takes a strong leader to do what isn't comfortable. I have been inspired by someone who I can relate to. I don't personally know this queen yet but I feel like our spirits are a-line together. When I hear her speak I get goose bumps. Almost every message she's shared I could relate to. Sarah Jakes Roberts impacts me by showing me I can be successful even though I had a baby at a very young age. I was 18 years old when I gave birth to my first child. Her name is Aaliyah. She's 11 years old now and she's as tall as me. Everyone reminds me everyday about how tall she is. I'm blessed to be a mom but it gets rough for me sometimes. I have to remind Aaliyah I'm new to being a mother for an 11 year old and you're new to being 11 years old so lets be patient with each other. I feel the battles of being a positive force of energy and resistance and the devil trying to kill, steal and destroy our joy. She reminded me to be the best version of myself. She exposed me to strong and powerful black women. She reminded me that as a woman I don't always have to have it figured out but if we let God lead us the lord will show us the way. SJR encourages me to keep fighting when it's hard, she can help you get your fight back. She cares about pouring into other leaders with her messages from God. That's the community. SJR show umjoa.

The goal is to develop leaders and not followers. The 21 irrefutable laws of leadership break this down beautifully in the chapter The law of explosive growth. " When you attract one follower, you impact one person. And you receive the value and power of one person. However, leaders who develop leaders multiply their organization's growth, because for every leader they develop, they also receive the value of all that leader's followers."- John C. Maxwell.

KUJICHAGULIA

Kujichagulia (Self-Determination): *defining, naming, creating, and speaking for ourselves*

2020 showed me more work opportunities in the virtual experience but I have to have self- determination. I experienced the world shut down for the first time. In person school classes closed and switched to virtual learning, jobs eliminated people fighting over toilet paper. But everything wasn't shut down. Technology thrived, technology increased profits and attention from the general population. I was introduced to the full virtual experience from me working from home because I lost my job due to the covid and my daughter's school being close and she doing school virtually. I definitely believe there are some small percentage of people already living like that because work from home and eLearning isn't necessarily new but for me and the culture of home schooling it wasn't common. I became my daughter's teacher assistant. Through that I notice that there are some additional lessons she could learn that I didn't see being taught. I created Riggs Academy.

Once I was completely exposed to the lifestyle I saw that life still moves on. Instead of in person events and workshops it was virtual and it still worked. People were still effective virtually. As long as you had the internet, a phone or computer, good lighting was set. You could even go to church in your living room or bedroom. Community can be formed virtually as well, that's what community showed me during and post pandemic The virtual experience has a con though and that is missing the face to face interaction with other people. So I just encourage you to not let the world shut down to stop you. If there is a will there's a way.

UJIMA

> *Ujima (Collective Work and Responsibility):*
> *building and maintaining our community*
> *—solving problems together.*

The deficit I see in today's culture is greed and not enough self-empowerment. I'm speaking from experience. I have worked for companies that care more about making money then developing leaders and caring for the unrepresented. It's enough money and resources for everyone. I think the greedy want to keep everything to himself, keep the poverty mindset amongst the people and break families of color down. There is power in our melanin and once you learn that you're dangerous. The insitiviates that I have been exposed to and a part of encourage the opposite. They promote unity and togetherness because with that we can start making change for a better tomorrow today.

UJAMAA

> **Ujamaa (Cooperative Economics):** *building and maintaining retail stores and other businesses and to profit from these ventures.*

I believe the misunderstanding between youth and adults is that the adults are set in their ways and the youth is stubborn. Depending on the generation of youth, the youth grew up in the technology era. Since the youth have been exposed to the internet and they know how to use it. We all have something to bring and offer- no matter if you're an adult or a child. The youth are stubborn because they think they know everything because of the internet. You can find anything on the internet. Just because you see it online doesn't make it the truth. Call me old school but I think the first teachers are the parents. But again, if our parents don't know how they can teach their families. We should be able to work together better as families. Better families create better communities. I think adults and youth can work together starting with communication. Creating productive brainstorming sessions, interactive activities can also build relationships between adults and youth and bridge the gap. It's important to listen and learn. It doesn't matter what age you can learn from someone.

Please share any research, projects, initiatives you have to share or things/ideas you are planning and visioning.

My aunt shared some information with me about Africa. I loved what I have researched: the culture, lifestyle, food. My goal is to build my dream home there and be a trailblazer for other young momtrepreneurs showing that anything is possible with the Rigg principles: realize your value, invest in yourself at the level you want a return, go for what you want, and get a dream team.

Lewis, Femi. "Kwanzaa: 7 Principles to Honor African Heritage." ThoughtCo, Dec. 17, 2020, thoughtco.com/kwanzaa-seven-principles-45162.

The Berkeley Well-Being Institute. 2022. Positive Affirmations: Definition, Examples, and Exercises. [online] Available at: <https://www.berkeleywellbeing.com/positive-affirmations.html> [Accessed 17 May 2022].

Indytenpoint.org. 2022. [online] Available at: <https://www.indytenpoint.org/> [Accessed 18 May 2022].

One United Bank. 2022. The History of Black Wall Street | One United Bank. [online] Available at: <https://www.oneunited.com/the-history-of-black-wall-street/> [Accessed 18 May 2022].

Crown Hill Neighborhood Association - Indianapolis. 2022. Crown Hill Neighborhood Association - Indianapolis. [online] Available at: <https://www.crownhillneighborhoodindy.com/> [Accessed 18 May 2022].

Adreonna Riggs is the owner of Riggs Consulting a business she started May 2020 after being laid off due to covid-19. Riggs Consulting provides administrative virtual assistant services such as cyber connecting, outbound calls, virtual event host, branding and project coordinating.

Before she became a full time entrepreneur she has spent 10 years in a variety of different customer service industry roles. Those positions and her dedication to the work allowed her to gain essential administrative, management and human resource skills she can use forever. She is also the treasurer for a nonprofit organization crown hill neighborhood association.

Adreonna's overall goal is to create thriving communities. She's passionate about helping individuals and families by being the gateway of resources. She is guided by the Rigg Principles: Realize your value, invest in yourself at the level you want a return, go for what you want, and get a dream team. She's born in Indianapolis, IN with hopes to expand to Africa summer of 2022 with her family. She currently lives with her 11 year old daughter Aaliyah who everyone reminds her that she's half her size already.

CIVILITY AND COMMUNITY

Thomas Dagwat Christian

Civility has always been in the center of the community because of its power for individual or corporate transformation and development. In the past, it was the nut tied on the bolt; but in recent times there has been a major shift from what used to be **CORE** in community building to what is now displayed in **MODERN** settlement.

This chapter seeks to return back to base the ideals/morals of the social relations, what/how communal living is today in Africa and beyond, social civility in leadership and some factors that are responsible for civility's balances and imbalances.

INTRODUCTION:

According to the MacMillan Dictionary (7th ed.);

Civility: is simply an art of politeness and positive social behavioral conduct.

Community: is a group of people living in the same geographical location that shares common ideologies, interest, attitude and culture etc.

I view civility as an act of genuineness and truth. While the community is one's circle of influence.

The lines in between these two terminologies and their dispositions intertwine greatly. It is premised upon the backdrop of civility that a society is built and sets to stride at all corners. It goes on to say that the human resources of a nation or state need to grasp an understanding of the concept of civility and its essence to manage any God-given natural resource.

According to Ivancevich and Glueck, Human Resource is the function performed in an organization that constitutes the most effective services of people (employees) to achieve the organizational and individual goals. While God-given Resources can directly be seen in the light of the Biblical scripture of Psalm 24: 1 that says *"The earth is of the Lord's and everything in it"*. These include – humans, animals, plants, waters, air, light, gold and so on.

Therefore, either as an individual or collectively, it is imperative that we understand the art of social intelligence with the aim of harnessing the society's potential. This is pertinent to nation building.

The esteem at which civility should be held in the community for social transformation cannot be overemphasized. Thus as humans, if we can leverage on the strength and power of civility, not just will our community be stronger and better, but families within a community could thrive on a smooth relationship with each. Individuals and organizations will experience the power of true transformation and positive societal development. We shall explore some factors that can lead to such an idealistic transformation and how it can transcend to community growth and development.

WHEN WE TALK OF THE COMMUNITY!

Oftentimes when the community is mentioned, it is always perceived in a broader sense of it; and when this happens, it gives a slim or no chance for an impact that could lead to transformation to revolve around and spread. It is almost the same as pouring a Bucket of water into a three (3) Ft. to thirty

(30) Ft. swimming pool and expects to swim inside. This would absolutely be impossible to achieve, don't you think so? It is true that when you have a wider scope of an idea such as the Community, making life's transforming impacts becomes heavy to achieve.

For example, in Jos, Plateau State – Nigeria; who's currently a 37-year-old youth has been running for the seat of the State Governor. He started expressing his political interest in his late 20s. He's failed woefully all the times he contested basically because of lack of capacity and resources. I met with one of his political campaign members and told him to relate to this vibrant and visionary young politician, to at least step down his political ambition to a more achievable position for now. He could go for the office of the Local Government Area Chairman or State constituency representation, but the highest position in the state is quite wide and colossal for him; especially for low capacity and minimum resources.

Young visionaries who have their communities at heart must have to accept the natural law of process and growth. There is nothing wrong about aspiring for our bigger dreams, but we can always remember to start with the mini-dream of the mega-dream and grow it into the level you envisioned. Maybe at this particular moment of life, you've got limited resources and capacity to aid the achievement of your bigger dreams. This may later not be a problem when you have appropriately developed our capacities and resources.

This is also related to civil community building. We all want to transform the community in which we live, right? Possibly you are like me who want to change the narrative of Gangsterism, drug abuse and Cultism in my locality, or make a life-changing impact in the lives of the homeless, widows and out of school children.

Here's how it starts!

Luke 14:28

For who would begin construction of a building without first calculating the cost to see if there is enough money to finish it? 29 Otherwise, you might complete only the foundation before running out of money, and then everyone would laugh at you. 30 They would say, 'There's the person who started that building and couldn't afford to finish it!' (NLT)

What is your capacity right now? What are your available resources? What level of life are you at? How emotionally or mentally strong are you to handle the storms of vision building? All these are some questions you should find answers to first before delving into impact making. Of course you may be a person of great faith and influence. There are exceptions to this school of thought.

I want to bring you closer to an idea of the community that will help you achieve your goal of community transformation. In a typical urban setting, let's say the first three (3) Houses by both sides of your home; first three (3) in front of yours and first (3) behind yours makes up your community in times of geography. This is to aid mutual understanding and maximum fellowship, because one of the features of an ideal community is its characterization of a warm embrace of fellowship.

I grew up in a typical rural community of Jos, Plateau State - Nigeria where there were only four houses in that location. I can categorically state that the only thing our parents never shared amongst themselves was their spouses, but almost everything was mutual to us living there.

It was an agrarian hamlet settlement that had existed for more than one hundred years. There was never a time that a family would lack anything basic to life and livelihood. If there was ever a lack for something, it was a lack for the whole community. My Late father had a Bicycle as the means of transportation for the whole village, our neighbor had a Television set; we all watched the Television together. The other neighbor was always having food and meat, we all ate as the community. The last family was good at farming, we all helped farm together, from one family to the other. I personally can sleep at any of the homes before coming to my house early in the morning and get ready for school.

Contrary to this fact stated, in this time and age globalization and urbanization factors have grossly contributed to the fading away of true communal living. For instance, it could seem like an integrity degradation for a person to request help from his or her neighbor. It is almost impossible to knock at your neighbor's house and request for a meal in peace and love. As a matter of fact, some people do not know the full name and nickname of their next door neighbor. In a city like Lagos, Nigeria; it is possible to live in an Estate with your childhood friend of years ago and not know you're in the same Estate until he's probably moved out. This is a true - funny and sad situation between my friend and his childhood friend.

Certainly this is not the ideal idea of the community God expects. God created man to be a social being and to exist in a community, with the aim of fellowship, communion, harmony and a frontier of reliability or trust for each other. One of the forehands of peace promotion is a communal living ideology and belief. The world is in a state of crisis because the human value system in the light of community is broken. Humans now live as strangers in a geographical location with fear, disunity, and distrust for each other. You can barely tell who's a friend and who's a foe!

Nations are against each other, social injustice, discrimination, modern settlement syndromes as well as competitive ideologies are all factors affecting the global peace of a community. The ever first story of jealousy, hatred and murder in the history of mankind recorded an incident that could be tagged 'you are you, I am me!' this is when an individual doesn't see/love his or her neighbor as would to his/her self.

Genesis 4:1-16

".......... When she gave birth to Cain, she said, "With the Lord's help, I have produced a man!" 2 Later she gave birth to his brother and named him Abel.

When they grew up, Abel became a shepherd, while Cain cultivated the ground. 3 When it was time for the harvest, Cain presented some of his crops as a gift to the Lord. 4 Abel also brought a gift—the best of the firstborn lambs from his flock. The Lord accepted Abel and his gift, 5 but he did not accept Cain and his gift. This made Cain very angry, and he looked dejected.

6 "Why are you so angry?" the Lord asked Cain. "Why do you look so dejected? 7 You will be accepted if you do what is right. But if you refuse to do what is right, then watch out! Sin is crouching at the door, eager to control you. But you must subdue it and be its master."

8 One day Cain suggested to his brother, "Let's go out into the fields." And while they were in the field, Cain attacked his brother, Abel, and killed him.

9 Afterward the Lord asked Cain, "Where is your brother? Where is Abel?"

"I don't know," Cain responded. "Am I my brother's guardian?"

10 But the Lord said, "What have you done? Listen! Your brother's blood cries out to me from the ground! 11 Now you are cursed and banished from the ground, which has swallowed your brother's blood. 12 No longer will the ground yield good crops for you, no matter how hard you work! From now on you will be a homeless wanderer on the earth."

13 Cain replied to the Lord, "My punishment is too great for me to bear! 14 You have banished me from the land and from your presence; you have made me a homeless wanderer. Anyone who finds me will kill me!"

15 The Lord replied, "No, for I will give a sevenfold punishment to anyone who kills you." Then the Lord put a mark on Cain to warn anyone who might try to kill him. 16 So Cain left the Lord's presence and settled in the land of Nod, east of Eden". (NLT)

Many crimes against God and humanity could be averted if individuals can perceive each other as one. Abel's blessings would've reached Cain if Cain had the right perception of a community. The belief of an ideal community is that of one for all, and all for one. It means that whatever causes joy to your neighbor, is your thing of joy as well; and whatever causes grief to your neighbor is your concern to grieve, and vice versa.

Growing up in the Northern Nigeria, I only heard of the great stories told by our parents about the good old days of communal living between the Christian faith and Muslim faith on the wider Jos, Plateau State - Nigeria. It is to that extend of not differentiating between Christmas celebration of the Christians and the Sallah (a celebration of the Muslim faith); because both parties were at every season commemorating it together for the interest of community peace. The sharing of food amongst each other, visitations and professional networking etc. Today, reverse is the case, this essential ingredient of peace stability is missing as there is a geographical separation for the Christian faith and Muslim faith. In some cases, both parties have rejected the gifts of food from each other. How sad it is!

Albeit, as previously seen in the definition of a community that; it is not just centered on a specified geographical location only, but can take other forms such as a group of persons with common ideology, interest, attitude and culture. A clear example of this school of thought is the collaboration of different authors to compile this monumental work for societal transformation. Such could be tagged as a community.

It goes on to say that at our various work stations and for as of endeavors can be a community even without that blood unifying factor. The Church and Mosque settings are a community. I so much love the way the Muslim community puts it. They call their community **"Umma(h)"**.

Umma(h) is an Arabic word for the Community of the believers and followers of Allah, it brings closer anyone who practices the faith of Islam into a warm circle of togetherness. As a theological concept, the umma(h) is meant to transcend beyond national, racial, and any classical divisions to unite all Muslims. The concept of the umma(h) dates to the time of the Prophet Muhammad and stresses the importance of the organization of society along ethical (and Islamic) lines (Source: en.m..Wikipedia).

The Christian faith and ideology of the community is not so far away from that of Islam. Just as how Dr. Mahamudu Bawumia (Vice President of the Federal Republic of Ghana) stated in his speech during the National Chief Imam at 100, A Birthday Breakfast/public lecture that took place on Tuesday 23rd April 2019 at the Movenpick Ambassador Hotel, Accra - Ghana that

"There is so much in common between Christians and Muslims than in difference".

In the Old Testament, God called the House of Jacob (Israelites) a community; He keeps on addressing thousands of people who are journeying together to the Promised Land, a Community. Coming to the New Testament, the believers of Jesus Christ's death and resurrection are referred to as a community of Christian.

Exodus 12:3

Announce to the whole community of Israel that on the tenth day of this month each family must choose a lamb or a young goat for a sacrifice, one for each household. (NLT)

As a matter of fact, during the early Christian persecution by the Emperor Nero in AD 64, the Christians were all living together in one unit at different locations; sharing in love everything worth sharing. This would later be the backdrop to the epistles of the Apostle Paul of Tarsus that largely culminates in the New Testament Bible of the Christians. (Source: Steve Gregg, Lecture Series on Church History).

God has always expected that Human beings would live as a community. He created human beings to be social beings and even some animals. God's creations can't exist without each other, and to exist with each other requires great social behavioral skill (Kenneth O. Gangel, Competent to Lead).

The differences in personalities, family orientation, ethnicity, socio-political interests, faith and beliefs systems need CIVILITY as a personal scoring skill for mutual acceptance and a peaceful co-existence. The home front is subject to this school of thought. Marriage involves two variants: individuals; this is the coming together of people with two different upbringings. It takes civility skill to build an ideal home.

LET'S GO TO AFRICA:

In Africa, the community is defined in a very broader perspective. It embraces far more than the nuclear and extended family systems. It cuts across ethnicity, culture and social identity. On a lighter mood, I've personally been introduced to some kindred by my Mother and when I became curious to ask about the channel of relationship no tangible words were given to me, I got to realize that My Mom had also been told by her Father about this seemingly distant relationship. Well that's how I will tell my kids about this kindred and the relationship continues.

Africa's grand belief of the community is that of "WE ARE ONE!" ideology irrespective of the thousands of ethnic-groups, clans, beliefs and nationals. According to Richard J. Gehman (African Traditional Religion 2001), there are approximately 1500 – 2000+ different ethnic-groups in Africa with different cultures and heritage. The philosophy that Africa has one Mother but different Fathers may be true in this sense, this is because of its vast similarities and intersections in values and beliefs all over the continent.

Firstly, the ancient African Traditional practice is the same all round throughout the continent. Approaches to the Supreme Being (Who is believed to be the Creator) may vary but the beliefs and dispositions remain the same. For example, I haven't seen an ethnic group, or a sect that has no Hospitality, Respect and Socialism as a core value to their culture/orientation in Africa. This is irrespective of the region and coast. The way of life and identity of the African man brings to mind the concept of civility.

Man as an individual is a modern idea to African culture or value, in the past; man was not primarily an individual but a member of a community. The family is extended. It included the brothers and sisters of parents with their families as well as grandparents. Sometimes the relationships between an Uncle and his nephew can be just as close as and even closer than between the actual parent and child.

In many cases, children are often closer to their grandparents than they are to their own parents, because the grandparents care for the children throughout the day while the parents are away working. Also, in the extended family, there is also a larger community of the clan and tribe. This is not limited to those presently within the geographical location and indigenous only, but even the foreigners amongst the community could be considered members of a family.

To be more emphatic, the family is the first place calling and duty of every man and woman, even the belief of Divinities have always had a link with the family systems. This is simply because the family is the first point of identity. Values, faith and culture, systems are first instilled in the family fora; when the family gets better, the society gets best!

In the early years of the South-African Post-apartheid, a renowned African Social Rights Activist and an Archbishop Desmond Tutu chaired the Truth and Reconciliation Commission in 1995, he created a profound philosophy which gained ground and served as the binding ring in South Africa and beyond.

The famous Ubuntu saying of the "I am, because you are and you are, because I am!" best explains the true underlying meaning of civility and community transformation. This comes from the school of thought that Humans cannot exist in isolation. We solely depend on each other's connections and care. Truth be told in this sense, like never before if there is a time that the world needs a conscious civility mindset in how we think and act about ourselves and towards others. This is because of the outbreak of the crisis state of the global nation. Worldwide we are faced with several leadership crisis, ranging from the home front, government, education, business world and what have you.

The exploitation of leadership has ruined the continent of Africa, to narrow in; Nigeria. Political leaders have little or nonchalant regard for their followers. They have line-up their own pockets and that of their close relatives at the expense of citizens.

The lifestyle of the leading elites is vastly different from that of those they lead. In most cases the saying that "power corrupts" has been more than fulfilled here. And I tell you this, that these conundrums of leadership and social injustice might not have an immediate solution because it has spanned across the borders of the supposed body of Christ which is the carrier of the solution. It seems like all hope is lost! Or has it?

The seemingly remedy is a more detailed understanding and deliberate attempt of civility.

When an individual is treated kindly, he or she would definitely have no option than to respond or give back kindly. Oftentimes the negative disposition of some persons in the society is a response to the negative imposition or influence on them. It goes rightly with 'Garbage in, garbage out". Just as how the Computer outputs on the inputs command of the operator, so also human beings are socially responsive to their influence.

The personality traits of a person, family/friend's circle and the community comes to form and shape the behavioral conduct of one in the society.

LEAD WITH CIVILITY

> *"Your legacy is created by how you treat others"*
> Shola Richards

A demonstration of genuine respect is a pathway every well-meaning individual should follow. People want to follow those they choose and not those they have to follow. Many times when the word leadership is mentioned most people's attention is swiftly drifted to a political or religious position. We are talking about community here, and the community is formed by families. So, let's bring in family leadership and civility to the front.

The first platform of leadership a young leader (child) learns leadership from and leads is in the home front. Also, parents have a direct and more day today leadership practice in the home than any other place of leadership. By this, it means that decisions and policies are made at home on a daily basis as a cordial relationship is concerned.

Leadership has to do with people! And people of different types and facets. Sometimes you just can't fathom when somebody is offended by your supposed innocent act. Politeness requires a gentle dialogue for the interest of peace and forgiveness. Even as a leader over a small or larger crowd, people must have to follow you because they choose to and not because they have to. A person can be positively transformed or inspired by your simple act of good.

A true leader is one who knows the way to inspire and influence others to follow in order to collectively achieve a set goal. He or she goes ahead to show the way and to inspire others to follow.

JESUS CHRIST IS THE PERFECT MODEL for this illustration. As Jesus made his way towards Jerusalem to be executed, the mother of James and John humbly requested that either of her sons be given a preferred seat next to Him in the kingdom of heaven. Both the disciples and their families have become so preoccupied with status rather than serving, they have missed the whole point of leadership. Jesus tells them plainly that the true model of leadership is that which stands in stark contrast to the words he teaches, that is; THE GREATEST MUST BE THE SERVANT. The Son of man came to serve and not to be served (Matthew 20:21).

As responsibilities increase, rights decrease. A civil/servant leader(s) knows that becoming a true leader of impact and influence begins by giving others their rightful privileges of glory. He or she is civil to consider the ideas of others in the team, which means that teamwork is required in leading with civility. They see feedback as a very good source of information whether positive or negative. When feedback is thrown at leaders, self-service leaders feel they are being attacked and threatened by followers. But a civil leader welcomes them and even desires to have it frequently to enable him/her to do better. As a result they are open to advice at all times.

While there are many qualities to look out for in a leader, one of the most fundamental factors to an influencing leader is the way he or she treats others. Leadership here is not necessarily premised on the position or rank one holds, but by the small or large influence one has on an individual or two persons or even a community.

> *"People will forget what you said, people will forget what you did, but people will never forget how you made them feel." Maya Angelou*

The best impacts are made when leaders lead with civility. It would be worthy of note that human beings are the disposition of their inside out as stated earlier. You are what you eat! Your social circle, preferred movies and songs all are factors that contribute to the person you are and will be. The positive or negative behavioral conduct of a person is not so far from his or her nurturing values and perceptions especially from the home.

Therefore, if we envisage an ideal community where all our hopes and dreams would actualize, family civility leadership must come to play a vital role in achieving this lofty aim. Parents or guidance must begin to teach their children or wards acts of respect and regards for humanity and society. Leadership is an act of guiding, coordinating a group towards a specific goal. (Bauta Moti)

It is an act of directing, helping, coordinating, influencing, motivating, and guiding a group to achieve their God giving purpose. Group here stands as a family or community. Today, can we begin to teach our kids civility in our homes? Only then will there be a promising great future for them!

The famous Maya Angelou's quote of "people will forget what you said, people will forget what you did, but people will never forget how you made them feel" is a typical calling for civility adherence. This goes on to say that the legacy of a person is linked to his or her civil abilities.

I've been a missionary to the streets and slum youths in communities and campuses for almost a decade. I answered the call immediately after my High School graduation at 17-year-old. It has been a lot of encounters and experiences all put together for my relevance in this generation. I've had tangible reasons to quit several times but often times when I check my Emails or text messages; simple words like "Thank you Thomas for coming my way today", dawn on me that God is creating a legacy for His glory.

As I approach old age and the end of life, I want to write a story to be left behind when I am gone. I once helped others find salvation in Jesus Christ and the purpose of existence in life.

However, when you lead a group, live something to be remembered as a memorial. Live a tangible element to be remembered. Jesus left the bread and the cup as symbols of the holy body and blood (1 Corinthians 11:24). You can also live with memorable words. It could also be an event or structure to be remembered or celebrated.

Corporate organizations have lost great potential that would have elevated an organization because of the Bossy act of incivility. Individuals have loose well-meaning friends by how they made others feel. As a person, civility skill is necessary for your relevance in life. You can become one who respects the wisdom of people even when you won't use it. Value people's roles and responsibilities in your life, home and workplace.

William Kamkwamba, is a Malawian inventor and an engineer who was the first person to build a windmill in his extremely poor village. At the age of 13-years, the uplifting journey of hope and perseverance led to a New York Times best-selling book. (Source: Boy who Harnessed the Wind, Kamkwamba and Mealer). Such true-life stories prove that wisdom could come from anywhere and anyhow.

The theory of civility says that as minor as the watchman security at your place of work may seem, he or she is very important as the Director General. So you don't just drive past him/her at the gate like he's a nobody.

What Civility Is:

- ➢ Civility is appreciating everyone's little or much contribution on the table
- ➢ Civility is consistently honoring others most precious resource 'Time'
- ➢ Civility is demonstrating trust in the ability of your team (family) members sometimes even when you know they won't deliver
- ➢ Civility is connecting personally to know what's going on with your team members aside your relationship
- ➢ Civility is that simple act of kindness that seems so small in times of need
- ➢ Civility is accepting differences and building strength on similarities.

All these outlined above are features of civility that can transform a community geographically and organizationally. But there's a big problem! The community TODAY is fractured with social vices/crime related activities of different types and facets in rural and urban areas across the globe. Around Nigeria, the most crimes are perpetrated by young people, due to the influence of illicit drugs and substance use, cultism and gangsterism.

It statistically accumulates that 9.7% - 10.4% of the populace uses drugs in Nigeria, Excluding alcohol and cigarette, with high prevalence from Northern Nigeria (Source: UNODC, 2017).

Also, about 10.5 million children between the ages of 5 - 14 years old are out of school in Nigeria. This represents 1/5 of all out of School children worldwide (Source: UNICEF).

In Northern Nigeria, almost half of the normal school age children are not attending any form of school formal education.

Many are unable to access classrooms or even obtain a quality elementary education. This pathetic situation makes children potential victims of Child labor, early childhood marriage, sexual violence, terrorism, kidnapping and other appalling societal threats.

Civil leaders are needed! I made up my mind to crusade on these vices bedeviling my community. I've lost friends and family members to the cold blooded murder of drugs, destinies and ambition have been cut short by the plights of today's youth. Would you lead with civility today? Let's make our communities great again.

Thomas Dagwat Christian is a dynamic Missionary of Christ, Human Capacity Builder and a Creative Strategist. He's a youth consumed by the fire and calling to help others find salvation and purpose of existence in life.

A must sought-after prolific speaker/trainer of contemporary Missions, Evangelism, Discipleship, Leadership and Purpose clarity; well known for combining Biblical truths with social issues and godly response.

He is the visioneer of GO Missions Network (a missions praying, mobilizing, training, sending & going agency) based in Jos, Nigeria.

Calls|WhatsApp|Telegram: +234 (0) 810 410 3078

Email: officialthomasjnr@gmail.com

MY COMMUNITY MY CULTURE

Blessy Iradukuna

Before going into detail, we begin to know what culture in general is and in particular Burundian community, which is ours. My community is defined and confined to my culture. The word "culture" is defined in different ways. Culture, in its broadest sense, is considered to be the set of distinctive features, spiritual and material, intellectual and emotional, that characterize a society or a social group. It includes, in addition to the arts and letters, lifestyles, fundamental rights of being human, value systems, traditions and beliefs. Human, value systems, traditions and beliefs. Human, value systems, traditions and beliefs. The French dictionary Larousse defines the word culture as being a set of material and ideological phenomena that characterize an ethnic group or a nation, a civilization, as opposed to another group or another nation. The French dictionary Larousse defines the word culture as being a set of material and ideological phenomena that characterize an ethnic group or a nation, a civilization, as opposed to another group or another nation. The French dictionary Larousse defines the word culture as being a set of material and ideological phenomena that characterize an ethnic group or a nation, a civilization, as opposed to another group or another nation. Here, the word culture has the same meaning as the word "civilization." Here, the word culture has the same meaning as the word "civilization." This same dictionary defines the word "culture" philosophically in three ways. First as the development of man's humanity through knowledge, then, in a social group, culture is the set of characteristic signs of someone's behavior (language, gestures, clothing, etc.) that differentiate him from someone belonging to another social stratum than him: bourgeois culture, workers. Finally, this word culture is the set of technological and artistic traditions characterizing this or that stage of prehistory. Let us start, as Lévi-Strauss himself does, from the classical definition of culture proposed by Edward B. Tylor: culture is "that complex whole that includes knowledge, beliefs, art, morality, custom and any capacity or habit acquired by man as a member of society" (1958: 1).

In particular, the Burundian culture we are talking about is the behavior of the first Burundians at home, in the neighborhood, in the family, , in the international community. This is due to an invisible mind that expresses itself in word and deed. All this, however, is given to man by the world, which finds it difficult or simple to make him brave, lazy, loves animals and farms, and gives him a thousand to build and make jewelry. Burundian culture provides mechanisms to avoid any language discrepancies. These are the methods of nonviolent communication and peaceful conflict management to the Burundian person. Anthropologist and Mushingantahe Zénon Manirakiza calls on all Burundians to avoid hate messages that are anti-values.

Indeed, when we talk about Burundian culture, we mean many things, that is to say those that characterize it. We quote among other things all these human values that we have cited above in the definitions of culture and the others such as dances and these are named according to the regions where they are practiced. There are cultural dances like Intore by Kirundo, Ingoma by Gishora, Agasimbo by Makamba, umuyebe, urwedengwe, amayaya, etc.

Among all these dances mentioned above and others that do not appear here because there are many, the one that is better known is the Ingoma of Gishora. This is considered as the country's heritage. In traditional Burundi, hunting was also practiced. What cannot be ignored is that Burundi has peculiarities in its culture. The example is the gender inequality we see in families. In Burundi, as in most other societies, culture assigns to girls and women different roles and functions than boys and men, and this creates unequal situations that hinder development. Gender roles in Burundian society are part of a very strong patriarchal culture. It is a patrilineal culture in which man embodies authority within the household, makes momentous decisions and provides the means of subsistence within the household.

As a result, Burundian women have no right of inheritance, no right of property and no right to control resources. The main responsibility of rural women is to cultivate the fields, raise livestock, collect water and wood, and take care of his family. These family and domestic responsibilities are often very heavy and leave him very little time to devote to income-generating activities.

Our culture is much broader because it tells us different socio-cultural characteristics of the Burundian peoples in their social diversity. As mentioned above, our culture is not limited to women. It also concerns the share of other genres and their activities, sometimes traditional or modern such as carpentry, masonry, hunting and many others.

Burundi is a constitutional republic whose second largest city, Gitega, became the political capital in 2019. Gitega is home to the Presidency of the Republic and the Senate, while the main state institutions are still based in Bujumbura, the economic capital.

Burundi's new constitution establishes the presidency of the republic of Burundi for a renewable term of seven years and creates the office of vice-president and prime minister. These three bodies constitute the highest authorities of the country.

The government's priorities are to fight against COVID-19; strengthening health services; to fight against corruption; revival of the agricultural sector; youth employability; and support for state pensioners.

Burundi has gone through a difficult economic situation over the past seven years, which has led to budgetary and balance of payments difficulties. To compensate for the loss of external resources, the Government mobilized internal resources, but this was not sufficient to meet a continuously rising social demand, driven by sustained population growth.

Economic growth was estimated at 1.8% in 2021 compared to 0.3% in 2020, supported by an easing of restrictions related to COVID-19. Economic growth is projected at 2.5% in 2022, supported by gains across all sectors.

Inflation remained high in 2021 at around 8.3% compared to 7.5% in 2020, driven by the rise in food prices and the monetization of the budget deficit. Inflation will remain high in 2022 at around 9%, particularly following the effects of the Russian-Ukrainian conflict on food and oil prices worldwide.

Being Burundian, we love our homeland at first sight and it attaches itself to its culture. We enjoy our culture and the way it accustomed us to being, to conduct us like the Burundian worthy of its name; it therefore prevents us from not dissociating ourselves from nature (the way of being). All over the country, all Burundians share the culture as we also share the language and we have almost the same way of approaching people when we express ourselves to them. For example, few of us Burundians speak aloud when we speak to someone asking for the floor, we seek to speak to him in a discreet way. And it happens even when these people are in the whole of the others, For this, we mean the linguistic value. Language is also part of culture, and for that matter; culture and language are intimately linked, because one cannot study the language of any country without studying its culture. In fact, "our language, Kirundi, is a powerful link and engine in the march of the revolution; we must discover it, penetrate it. "

What cannot be ignored, is that even if in Burundi Ancient was not observed by writing (lack of books to keep what is said), this phenomenon did not prevent anything because when we have the desire to advise, prevent or warn, etc. someone else, we had the other way to talk to him what we want to say. Ancient Burundi, as was the case for all of Africa in general, was located in a civilization of orality where speech was of paramount importance. The word had a strength and had the value of an act. It was a factor of social integration or disintegration. In Burundi in particular, in the context of cultural and linguistic homogeneity, the language (Kirundi) had crystallized in certain literary works that Burundians shared while they went about their daily activities. We find this cultural, literary and artistic richness in this quote from Emile MWOROHA when he says: "Basically, the Burundian people can boast of having forged not only an old state but above all a living and beautiful culture. This culture is popular, expressed essentially in the Kirundi language, in the poetry in the broad sense that the Burundian mountaineer enjoyed in the pieces dedicated to bees, cows going to the trough, the grain that is pounded, the churn or iron ores that melt, the fish of the rivers, the hero of yesteryear, the friend met, to the hare or bush leopard.

That is why we have said that the language in general and in particular the Kirundi language occupies an important place in Burundian culture. These literary traditions of ancient Burundi that we have said above are based on a frequent and artistic use of the phenomenon of Ijambo. In this culture of orality, we find a solidarity of the link that exists between man and his word. Its social role of speech is one of the essential characteristics of African civilizations in general. For example, in this regard, the Burkinabe historian Joseph Kizerbo writes: "In short, speech is a dialectical process between biology, techniques but through the mediation of the group. Without an echoing partner, without interlocutors; man would be mute but reciprocally the word is such a precious achievement that in magical or cosmogonic African representations, magical or Cosmogonic Africans, we recognize him a grip on things. The verb is creative. Speech is also the vector of progress. It is the transmission of knowledge, tradition, or the inheritance of the ears. It is the capitalization of knowledge that definitively raises man above the eternal mechanical class of instinct. At the end of the dawn of social authority, that is, leadership and power, was made. » In Burundian culture, the genius and the art of speech are found in the words of traditional Burundian literature. In this literature, we noted the poetry sung and told which has an essentially artistic function with the elegance of the towers and the cleverly arranged play of words. Not only the sung poetry but also we will note the sung and danced music that makes the zither (inanga) speak Finally, it is the role of tales, fables and legends with mythical characters (the giant ogre: igisizimwe) or the interventions of SAMANDARI and INARUNYONGA.

In an article Fleuve long abondant comme l'eau, entitled Literary traditions musical compositions and rural development in Burundi, Adrien NTABONA highlights the osmotic character of this traditional literature of Burundi, that is to say link between this traditional literature and everyday life. Here's how he puts it: "In Burundian translation, literary productions and cultural expeditions have played a leading role in motivating the socio-economic activities of the rural world. And this in the most varied forms: sometimes they were songs in Solon, sometimes they were popular rondeaux based on dialogue between a soloist and a choir and between two choirs; sometimes they were lyrical recitations accompanied by a musical instrument(inanga, ikembe, umuduri, idonongo) sometimes they were eloic and pastoral recitatives based on declamation, incantation where solons take vigor and melody. »

All this literature was inscribed in everyday life and sought to give it meaning. In this way, there was a connivance and interconnection between literary production and daily activity to the point that one could speak of osmosis. The set of recitatives and songs related to agriculture, to animal husbandry, hunting, beekeeping and pastoral incentives, for example, it should be noted in summary that the human values that emerged from them were, first, the self-sufficiency of households in matters of food whatever the activity, then the love of work, thirdly work in common, fourthly work as an expression of communion with nature and finally fidelity to the invisible world. In other words, Burundian culture Burundian culture and especially that of ancient Burundi could be inserted into what we call literature. And this traditional literature by its substance as in its form has interested more than one specialist. Among the latter, we count missionaries who have published works resulting from the collection campaigns, namely proverbs, tales, legends, myths, epics, riddles, riddles of songs, etc. The situations of communication that are at the basis of the production of literary texts later in Burundi are numerous; these are, for example, ordinary situations in situations of simple exchanges, during many family celebrations, at birth, at weddings, on the occasion of death, around work or in a situation of rest and we have the typology of different discourse.

Among other things, we have allative speeches that are speeches that have in common public words. this is called Ijambo or "prayer" intended to praise someone. Today, we can add scientific speeches or public lectures. In addition, there are appellative or onomastic discourses (related to nouns), that is to say it is any discourse with an appellative function. We know, for example, that in Burundi old when there was a newborn, to name it depends on the circumstances in which the child was born. We can mention names like NYANZIRA when the delivery of this child was happening on the way, BACAMURWANKO or RURIHOSE when in the neighbors there are disagreements, names like NZANIYABANDI when the parents of the born child give birth and the children die on the day of delivery or after a few days from birth, names like NTAHONKURIYE when the child's family is surrounded by enemies, killers, etc. This phenomenon is also observed even today, even if it is rare. This name did not only concern people, but also places. After the speeches of appellation, we observe desiccant speeches. As the name suggests, these are the speeches by which the speaker expresses a wish or desire, a wish. We still observe this kind of speech ibitutsi, imisibo or incomprecations (hurtful words) and swearing (indahiro) or greetings.

In Burundian culture, the one who is granted something presents praise to the one who gives it a gift. Hence the laudatory speeches; either the proclaiming laudatives (the proclaimed words) or the citatory laudatives (the sung words) in these first, they are classified: the auto panegyric (ivyivugo), the bucolic (ibicuba), the hunting (amahiga), the apical georgic (amavumbi or amayuki), the odes of the cultivator (amazina y'isuka) especially during the practice of the countryside; ikibiri in Kirundi. And in the second, there are lullabies (ibihozo), laments (intimba). As an example, we heard a person talking about coherent words either by simply speaking. Either by singing at the party when there was absolute silence or during the night on mountains. It was claimed that the person was abnormal. In addition, there are narrative discourses or dialectics that are the stories, fables or fabliaux and chronicles. There were also normative or sententious discourses that required norms or that elicited advice such as webbeds (imyibutsa), prohibitions (imiziro). After that, came speeches by which we tried to impose by the word a certain behavior. There are among others incantations (imihamuro or imitongero), blessings and curses. For a long time, no one owned everything. That is why the one who wants something from someone else accepts to bend over by praying to him. This kind of discourse is called the precative discourse. People met in privileged spaces (example around the fire) to relax and have fun. They were hours of riddles, riddles, laughter and humor, tellurisms (imyigovyoro). These kinds of speeches are called recreational because they were said at the end of activities, or even at rest. It was in these speeches that advice or information was given for a child who was lazy or who did not follow the family's orders.

In ancient Burundi, at certain times of the day and especially in the evening in particular So as has already been announced, the word had great importance in Burundian culture; hence there is much more talk for linguistic culture.

So, it was by word that we warned someone or tried to give them advice, etc.

Burundian culture and not only this one but also other cultures of the world are at the heart of contemporary debates on identity, social cohesion and the development of a knowledge-based economy. So, as has already been mentioned in the definition of culture, it is the set of different traits that man entails. Among these traits, we return to value. One can collect from the latter; a kind of ideological concept of rules, of morality to which one is attached. It distinguishes the values common to a group of people, to a community and the values specific to a person. We can refer to this quote from Cornelius' Cid saying "To well-elderly souls value does not wait for the number of years". For this element of culture that is value, we imply three types that are first of all human values which are in turn those that allow us to show our humanity, that is to say our feelings of respect, consideration, appreciation and empathy. For other humans. Secondarily, come the ethical values which are those that enact conduct that respects others and does not harm them. We can add that respect for animals as well as plants is also part of it. Finally, we evoke the moral values that are those that are prescribed by our religion or that we attribute to ourselves. These are the laws, rules and external injections. These values prescribe the conduct of respect on the other of his physical and mental integrity, of his life. Moral values are often associated with major religions such as Christianity, Islam, Buddhism or ideologies that are inspired by political systems.

It is important to analyze the value system that prevails in each society and the majority of these values are reflected in the traditional culture of each person. For their transmission (these values), the school and the family remain the main channels of transmission for the acquisition of these values by young people. However, among the important ones of this system of values are respect for life, the spirit of tolerance or understanding of the other, the spirit of solidarity, fairness or sharing, the sense of responsibility and benevolence, fidelity to the word given, patriotism and many others. Basically, what we can remember about Burundian culture is to take by heart valiant all these values that the individual entails because they are what distinguish him from an animal. And we must not acculturate Burundian culture by mixing it with other foreign cultures, under the pretext that we are modern and moreover losing culture is like losing its identity. It is said in Kirundi: "UWUTAYE AKARANGA ABA ATAYE AKABANGA!"; at least it is he who does not have culture and is not far from the tree that has no root.

On the other hand, Burundian culture allows us to achieve these on the one hand and on the other hand, there is another that this culture hinders us from accomplishing not for the will but for the law. Hence the impacts related to this culture. Burundian culture influences us to respect others. The example is for children. A child must obey his parents and any other who is superior to him. For a long time, a child could not make movements back and forth when his father is eating, or even today when we pass very close to the one who is eating, we do not feel comfortable. We feel ashamed. The worst is when the person in question is older. This behavior is drawn from Burundian culture. It is the same that when an elderly person or an authority speaks, everyone around him pays attention by lending him an ear. Here we can understand that culture teaches us to display respect first for oneself and then for others. Burundian culture influences us in the way of our clothing, in the way of our production of speech, whether in a lot of people, or in a discreet place. As for the outfit, nowhere will you find a Burundian who goes for a walk with clothes that show his nudity or any other bad behavior in relation to it. We have already seen that the word has a great importance in Burundian culture. A Burundian does not know how to speak aloud when he wants to address someone, he warns him or away from others to tell him or beg him for something. Dances, music and other artistic kinds challenge us to keep our culture. For example, some traditional dances or music challenge how young girls can behave before or after marriage and/or they can conduct themselves in front of their husbands or in-laws when they are in the home. To say that these dances and music contribute a great thing to Burundian education. Not only the traditional music and/or dance that constitutes Burundian culture but also modern music is part of it. When modern music or modern dance is outside Burundian culture, it would not be produced on Burundian territory. Anyone can boo it by saying that the one who produced it is out of Burundian culture. The recent example, we have heard or seen through the radio or social networks the abolition of some songs like ibisusu, etc. under the effect that the producers of these songs do not respect Burundian culture. Referring to Burundian culture, there are words and/or acts related to these words that are not allowed to speak aloud or when one wants to address a large number of individuals. Words that are related to sex, are considered taboo. Other words or deeds that are not allowed to be carried out at the understanding or sight of others are those of doing the great need or small need. It is shameful to see someone who is defecating very close to the path or in the whole of others if only if it is abnormal. We saw what happened to the one who was photographed being defecated in the bush. Hence the Ministry of Culture, which takes care of everything. is related to culture. This is the reason why we have that Burundian culture impacts us to make ourselves respected and to respect others.

However, Burundian culture hinders us much more from flourishing. With modernity, one would have to be stripped of seniority and one acquired novelty. As we have pointed out earlier, Burundian culture considers sex education to be taboo. Parents do not dare to talk to their children about what is related to sex. They see themselves as the promoters of the loss of culture. But with globalization, we are witnessing the mixing of culture. Today, we attend television, we make trips from Burundi abroad, we use the telephone (use of social networks: internet) and other movements. Not only that but also currently, there is the school where the not bad designers of the books are the foreigners and these first to realize their fact, they insert their culture because we said that culture and language are linked. So, the child draws from here and there, that is to say what has seen play or go through the television or what has read on the book and/or the internet, and then he wants to imitate it by implementing it. That is why parents could not remain silent, they could make allowed what is taboo by still referring to culture. Of course, Burundian culture influences us not to acquire the other languages well besides our language, Kirundi. We know that to learn, we dare to speak out loud while Burundian culture challenges us to speak in a low voice with what we can say in Kirundi "ubupfasoni". So, we do not flourish to acquire these languages. Note also that to learn a language, you must also learn the culture of the country concerned. For a Frenchman, to say in his language "the vagina or penis" in all the others, for him it is easy but for a Burundian who is learning French, to produce these words in French, he always thinks that he is committing a crime because he knows them in his mother tongue and that this language does not allow him to speak words like that. So he doesn't feel comfortable.

So, even if our culture influences us to non-fulfillment, it helps us overcome some challenges or any other that surrounds us. In Burundian culture, the practice of marriage had existed for a long time. Families gave themselves children even today, this fact still exists. Nowhere is it heard that the brother marries his sister or the uncle marries his niece or other such relationships. But elsewhere, we can witness the marriage of children who share the same parents. Burundian culture still practices incest, what is called in Kirundi "IKIZIRA". And besides, it's incest anyway why because it's shameful to see or hear the brother who married his sister. If this were the case, this is where there would be inbreeding for the children they would be getting.

95

Even more, there are many challenges that Burundian culture helps us overcome. We have already mentioned that not having the culture is like a tree that has no root. Because a tree that is not in possession of the roots cannot exist. The technological world has evolved, different cultures go through television or the Internet. Currently, in the world, we do not know that these are the moments that end. We hear about marriages that are performed for people who have the same sexes, from which it has been said that cultures differ; but Burundian culture does not allow us to do this type of marriage. Burundian culture does not allow us to eat anything as we observe in our neighbors the Congolese who can eat caterpillars, lizards, to name but a few. Burundian culture therefore invites us to respect and protect nature.

We could refer to our government, when we say the government we could understand any head of state, what existed and what still exists (those who are already dead and those who are alive). Why because they are the ones who have set up the Ministries in general that challenge the population to respect or practice Burundian culture and the Ministry of East African Community Affairs, Youth, Sports and Culture which is responsible for guaranteeing Burundian culture, that is to say, the ministry that keeps the non-violence or no Burundian culture. For example, our Head of State, who is currently in power in collaboration with the Ministry of Culture, Youth and External Relations, often organizes youth forums through which we observe dances, music, poetry and prayers (lyrics) that challenge young people to follow Burundian culture. Even more, the Head of State in collaboration with the Ministry of the Environment, Agriculture and Livestock have set up to protect the environment by planting trees in the project called in Kirundi "EWE BURUNDI URAMBAYE" and the protection of the land by drawing hedges that slow down the waters for the great mountains by fighting against erosion. From here we understand culture through respect for nature. Fortunately, Burundians are used to greeting each other when they cross paths or meet each other at home. But they greet each other in different ways, either by giving each other a hand, or crossing each other very close or by saying amahoro only, and raise their hand when you are far away. This habit still exists at this time. So, during or after the pandemic, our culture played a big role. For example, for this recent pandemic that still exists "COVID-19", because we are already used to using the greeting of AMAHORO, it was very easy for us during this pandemic, we use this type of greeting or that of raising our hand.

In fact, what is lacking in the current Burundian culture is the lack of respect for oneself and others. Because of globalization, there is the mixing of cultures. So, there is acculturation. Sometimes we see men straightening their hair, which is intended for women. Today's population has made applicable what is forbidden in ancient Burundi. We want to ally ourselves with foreign cultures. For example, when a Burundian travels to Rwanda or Tanzania, after a few weeks, we hear him talk about ikinyarwanda or Kiswahili. He cannot accept that he is Burundian. A Burundian who travels changes any behavior that makes him a Burundian. There is a need for improvement from teaching related to Burundian culture through television or either radio and the Internet and then in schools, it is necessary to insert programs related to Burundian culture and not foreign culture.

The other element that shows that there is a deficit in Burundian culture that cannot be ignored is that women want to consider themselves as men. We understand here that women want there to be gender equality, which Burundian culture does not allow them. Women want them to be inherited like men. Since ancient Burundi, the woman received what is called in Kirundi "IGISEKE". These women imitate other foreign cultures while each culture is built in its own way of organization. For young people, we must follow the orders and advice given by our parents or superiors. The disagreement between young people and adults is that the former want to be free by allying themselves with foreign cultures because they are born in modernity where there are televisions, radio, the use of the Internet, etc. young people want to copy these cultures and have them brought to Burundi. When their parents promulgate advice to them or when they tell them how they behaved in ancient Burundi, young people say that they are in democracy, so that they are in modernity.

In short, what we need to do cannot abolish all these features of modernity, but we need rules to follow to keep our Burundian culture. The government must implement the policy of broadcasting soap operas on radio and television that challenge people burundian culture and on the Internet, we need sites that publish what is related to the latter while inserting the elements we have seen such as fables, riddles, songs with instruments like umuduri, ikembe,... so that the culture remains with a flavor. Soon, we could not know what the riddle is, even now we do not find anywhere where this kind of question appears in national competitions.

So the best solution is for adults and young people to get together to discuss Burundian culture. Adults can hear young people and understand them. In fact, adults should challenge young people about the values that govern man and young people would compare what they watch on television or at different sites with those told by their superiors. In a single word, it is important to have an understanding between adults and young people and we must keep our culture because we can draw from this Kirundi adage of our great parents who says: "UWUTAYE AKARANGA ABA ATAYE AKABANGA!" In English "those who throw away are throwing away!"

Blessy Iradukunda
+257-7235-0375

My dream is that one day I will be able to serve children/orphans and widows in my country, Burundi.

High School Certificate, Blue Lakes International school; P. O Box 2862 Kigali – Rwanda; Class of 2020

Public Relations Officer/Interpreter;

NT Global Solutions & Nambiar Associates, Bujumbura, Burundi

Work with different company's departments with my main responsibilities being:

- Representing my company in professional meetings and providing interpretation when required;
- Marketing company's products, such as FingerPrints & Camera Surveillance;

- Translating internal documents from English to French & vice versa ; and
- Contributing in answering and providing information regarding the company's products to customers.

Member of SYD Family (Signboard of Youth Destiny); Bujumbura, Burundi/ Kigali, Rwanda

SYD vision is to transform, upskill, and empower African youths into better citizens and leaders. As part the team, I participate in:

- Providing basic needs for vulnerable children and their families;
- Inspiring young people to be exemplary leaders in their communities; and
- Supporting vulnerable children to access quality education.

Member of BlessedGirlsTeam; Bujumbura, Burundi Nov.2020-To Date

BlessedGirls is an association of helping girls in different ways, like physically and spiritually. And our vision is to see our girls shining, excelling in their future. And as a member of the team i participate in the following :

- Providing some materials and basics needs to our girls;
- Inspiring and encouraging them to get their voice, and to know their values;
- To share the Gospel and the goodness of our Lord.

School Counselor; Primary School, Le Sourire, Ruyigi, Burundi

Le Sourire is a school that promotes rights to quality education for all, especially orphans and street children. My work consists of:

- Assisting in School orientation and welcoming newcomers; and
- Counseling children with depression.

Guide/Interpreter; Burundian Football Federation

- Volunteer in the Burundian's Football federation where I provide guide and interpretation services to footballers from other countries coming to play in Burundi.

COLORING WITH GOD

Jenny Cupp

"Artists are just children who refused to put down their crayons" - Al Hirschfield

In the beginning there were Crayola crowns that's how I pronounced them but actually it was Crayola crayons. I loved to draw starting around five years old. Lots of paper and coloring books and sidewalks. I would take some of my broken crayons and put them on the driveway in the sun and let them melt.I would blend them together and create . It parlayed into drawing fashion and making paper books with my mom. We would spend hours together drawing and making things.

My mother and her father were oil painters, artists, entrepreneurs and were involved in the theater. This included acting, costume design and set design. My grandfather owned a gift store called "Foxes" after his last name. It was an eclectic combination of gifts, greeting cards, paintings and antiques. My mother followed in his footsteps and opened an antique store called "The Cellar Door". She would trash pick from what people were discarding and go to the dump finding treasures. She would refurbish furniture and bring things back to life with her creativity. I was surrounded with creativity and I was always encouraged to draw. My mother worked for a photographer and was commissioned to hand paint the photos to give them color. Her easel and paints were set up in our living room. I believe I was around five years old and got into my mother's paints. I managed to make a big mess on the carpet and myself - I remember being punished and that ended my chance to paint with my mother. My mom decided to teach my older brother how to paint and sent me to ballet school. My calling as a painter was thwarted at a young age, but I continued to draw and loved making art and listening to music together.

When I was 13 my mom died from cancer. It shook my entire being.My brother had come home from college and I thought it was for Thanksgiving a time of celebration with family around the dinner table, a tradition. My mom had been in the hospital for months this last time. I would ask my dad how my mom is and he would say "she is not getting any better". In my mind I thought ok she is staying the same and they are trying to help her. No one ever said she is dying. On Thanksgiving morning my brother came into my room and woke me up. He told me our mom died.I had not seen her because she wanted me to remember her healthy and not in pain. I was being protected but in the end I was in shock, we were extremely close. . I spent a lot of time at friends' houses because my Dad worked full time. But my time home alone was spent sorting through my thoughts .Losing your mom at any age is difficult. I would sit in my room for hours listening to music and Joni Mitchell was one of my favorites to draw to. Sitting on the floor and drawing with a split quill pen and black India Ink. It was my escape and expression in black and white. I loved that she was moody and extremely poetic. Her voice was ethereal yet strong and she was an artist. I would get lost for hours creating. It gave me peace and a closeness to my mom

"Oh, I am a lonely painter
I live in a box of paints
I'm frightened by the devil
And I'm drawn to the ones that ain't afraid'
"I remember that time you told me, you said
"Love is touching souls"
Surely you touched mine
Cause part of you pours out of me
In these lines from time to time"

Song Lyrics   Joni Mitchell   A case of you

" Blue, songs are like tattoos
  You know I've been to sea before
 Crown and anchor me
 Or let me sail away"
 "Hey Blue, there's a song for you
  Ink on a pin
  Underneath the skin
   An empty space to fill in
    Well there's so many sinking
    You've got to keep thinking
    You can make it through these waves"

Song Lyrics   Joni Mitchell   from the song Blue

> *"Art washes away from the soul the dust of everyday life"* **Pablo Picasso**

I started to write poetry and created books of illustrated poems. This was also the time period in Highschool when I started making jewelry. Mostly beach and ocean themed pieces. I loved collecting seashells and beach glass and puka shells from Hawaii. The Puka shells were white round shells with holes in the center popular with the surfing culture and most of my friends surfed. I loved creating my own designs with seashells .I grew up on the beach in Cape May NJ. A Victorian seaside town with gingerbread architecture. Our family spent every summer there and when I was little we stayed with my grandparents ,my mother's parents. They had a house in an area called Fishing Creek a little distance from Cape May. A lot of our relatives lived around us .I have great memories of singing around the piano and at the dinner table at my grandparents' house. Eventually we purchased our seaside home in the heart of Cape May blocks from the beach and boardwalk. We had large family gatherings at the beach and if you weren't family you became family. We were a tribe of laughter and music and love.

This is my mom on a Cape May postcard

My mom and I at the beach

I have always and always will live near the ocean. It is my place of peace. It is where I talk to God a lot and glean from for inspiration. The colors of the sea and sunsets are all around . This theme of waves and water and storms and empty boats has repeated throughout my life in my artwork.. and in my life.

"Some people look at a puddle and see an ocean with ships" Zora Neale Hurston

Shells and feathers and driftwood were my Art supplies . It is here I want to encourage you to look around you. There is much to create with. It does not require expensive art supplies to be a creator. With my jewelry I upcycle and recycle. I take broken pieces and make something beautiful. I use what has been discarded and broken and recreate and give it new life. Even beach glass was once tossed into the ocean as trash. Over time the tossing in the waves and stormy seas brings forth a weathered treasure. There's a key right there and for me something generational. Taking trash and bringing forth something beautiful like my mother did.

I moved to California when I was 18. Just leapt out with my tattered wings and a prayer .

I landed a job making and designing jewelry and being mentored in all things retail. I had a woman ,my boss, who saw my potential and she sowed into me. I became a buyer and a freelance window dresser. I was self-taught but had an eye for design from the environments I grew up in. I did all the fashion ads drawing them for the store so everything I did as a child became my career. I had two years of junior college and took all the art classes I could take. One of the things that birthed out of school was an art show I had in downtown Santa Cruz. I had created handmade ceramic masks /faces. All my life experiences and gained knowledge started to fit together and build my career.

We do not necessarily all learn through traditional schools or traditional materials. This is where you should look around you and access resources from your surroundings. Pursue the things you love doing, things you have a natural inclination for. What brings you joy while doing it?

I met my fiancé in California. I moved to Colorado with him because he got a job offer and I was in love and we got married. Colorado was beautiful with mountains and lots of snow and skiing but I always felt like a fish out of water without the ocean. We returned to California after a couple of years. Sadly, my marriage did not work out and I returned back to New Jersey broken-hearted. I had to leave California and my friends and the job I loved and start all over creating a new life.

Some of our most powerful and beautiful creations will come out of our broken places. I encourage you to express it all, be transparent, it will not be all joyous expressions if we are honest. There are those needing to know there is "beauty from ashes" That good and beautiful things come out of desolate places.

Isaiah 61:3 "And to provide for those who grieve in Zion to bestow on them a crown of beauty instead of ashes, the oil of gladness instead of mourning, and a garment of praise instead of a spirit of despair." NIV Bible

I had a pivotal encounter with the Lord after crying out to him. I cried "if you're really real I need you now! This was during the time my marriage was coming apart. My brother was struggling with some issues back East, in New Jersey, so I decided to return home. Before I left California in the store where I worked, two women came in. The one woman came up to me and said "There's some things the Lord wants me to say to you". She had my attention and basically she told me "this is your life" she explained every detail down to my mother's death. This is a whole other story actually one of my testimonies to be written but this was the day I asked Jesus into my heart and became Born Again. I left behind years of soul searching, New Age beliefs and a lot of deception. It was a life changing decision and would birth out my God given destiny as an artist for the Kingdom of God.

When I moved back to New Jersey I looked into and worked at a hair salon. I decided to take the receptionist job and observe. I liked that it is creative and helps people feel good but I realized my back issues would not allow. I had injured my back in Colorado and had a disc injury.

Creativity can be expressed in so many ways. There's really no limitations, no borders or boundaries to creativity. No right or wrong or perfect way, just freedom in the flight of your brush or the scissors in your hand.

My brother was successful with his Ballroom dancing although he started late age wise for dancing; it came naturally to him. Interestingly, as kids my mom sent me to ballet school and taught my brother how to paint. Later in life we both stepped into our rightful streams of creativity. My brother and his partner became National Ballroom Champions two years in a row. They had put together a showcase of champions I remember watching from the balcony crying thinking what a legacy my mom and grandfather left behind. He began producing shows and asked me to do the costuming. It was a cast of 25 people and set in the roaring twenties. I never sewed but my creative side said I can do this. I was excited by the challenge. I went to thrift stores and found dresses that could be changed, embellished and transformed. I did the same thing for the men's costumes. I found fedora hats for the men but not the hats for the women so I made them. I loved making them with beading and feathers. It felt as though I had always made them. I designed all the jewelry and put together the full outfits. It felt so natural and I was so inspired by the challenges. I worked with a seamstress to redesign the dresses and was a wardrober for the shows helping with costume changes. I later found out my great grandmother was a milliner. Historically milliners imported an inventory of

garments and sold them in their millinery shops. Many milliners worked on both milliner and fashion designing such as Coco Chanel. I love how all of our history comes into play if we let it. I was happy to be in the background creating.

I did a couple more fine life productions with my brother but then eventually returned to retail. I opened and created a store for a gentleman and ran it for a couple of years. I was given the freedom to design the logo and store design and do all the merchandising. I eventually left there and moved into a

111

woman's boutique and was there for 17 years. I was the manager, buyer, merchandiser and the personal stylist to my clients. I continued to make jewelry and sell at various locations including my own pop up stores and was still freelancing window dressing. I always worked hard and my total years in retail was forty years. I was a surfer (started surfing at forty) and rode my bike everywhere but the lifting and physical parts of retail had a cost and I herniated 3 discs. Because of my back I lost my job and during this time my dad died. Everything was crashing down. I ended up in my bed in my living room for a year. Unable to sit, I could only lie down or stand briefly. I felt like I was in the wilderness-a storm at sea but keeping my eyes on Jesus was what carried me.

It was testing time. I lost everything, my job, my insurance, my freedom from being bed bound. Most painful was my dad dying during this time. I was in so much physical pain I was unable to mourn his loss till latter. I kept praying and questioning myself and God. At one point I heard the Lord say you are three quarters of the way through. As if I would come out the other side I grabbed a hold of this like a life raft.

I was starting to be able to stand more. One day the Lord spoke to my Spirit in a still small voice and said " I want you to paint white on black because I Am the Light in the darkness." I found these black shopping bags from my job that I had accumulated. I found a paintbrush and some white paint in my Jewelry and craft supplies. I taped the bags to my wall and about 10 paintings came out in the next few days. I would stand and paint. Remember I have never painted before. Again a still small voice said "You're gonna go up front and go bigger. What? Who am I? What does that mean? No, my brother does that, not me. I had no idea what that meant but I was fearfully trusting Him.

Creating art and being a co-creator will stretch you way way way beyond your comfort zone. You will be pushed out of your comfort zone and in my case never to return. You have the choice to fall or fly and the chance to flap your wings whether you jump or get pushed. I recommend flying.

The Lord started opening doors for me to paint at churches and meetings and the invitations kept coming. I have never asked to paint, I will make myself available but He opens the doors.

I got invited to a church to paint every Sunday with the worship team. I can't help but think of being in my room drawing to music. The Lord had already put in place a foundation in my childhood "all things work together for our good" I eventually started teaching prophetic painting to children and adults through our Kingdom Impact school. The Lord called me out to other churches and then to conferences. I had to trust fully in His leading even down to the color paints I would pour. I was still and still am painting only on black boards but now with all different colors. There are many times when I have no idea what I am going to paint till I am in front of the easel. This keeps me dependent upon Him. I count it all joy.

I remember talking with my dad one time and he shared with me that my mom used to paint on stage while her father talked and lectured about painting .How beautiful that my destiny all along was to paint with my father (God) while he speaks. Eventually the Lord would have me share the words that were with the paintings and He would highlight who I was to give the painting to. Now I open my mouth by invitation and share what the Lord is giving me to everyone. It is an honor and joy and Holy to paint prophetically. I always say I get to color with God ..the king of kings!

I was invited to paint at a church and the speaker (awesome man of God) Kris Miyaki stood up to speak. He turned to me and said "Jenny, when you paint a lot of arrows are shot at you but the Lord wants you to know that he covers your organs with his hands. You pull out the arrows that are on your sides and you flip them over and dip the feathers in the paint and paint with them . This is your warfare, this is your worship!

Psalm 144 "Praise the Lord who is my Rock He trains my hands for war and gives my fingers skill for battle" NLT Bible

During Covid and being in lockdown became rich soil to grow from. My jewelry making was a no-brainer. I spent hours building my inventory of prophetic and one-of-a-kind pieces that I prayed over but I missed painting. I whined to the Lord and said "Lord I miss painting during Worship". I miss painting in a church and conferences and ministering. In His own still small voice He said to me "well set up your easel in your living room and put on worship music and paint ! What a concept I never painted at my house except in the very beginning on those black bags, amazingly obvious but it never crossed my mind. So during Covid in my house it was all different.. heavenly angels being released and captured in paints and on canvas. Now with time and worship came revelation and reflection. A whole different level. I would paint during prayer by myself and with other intercessors on the phone. I believe I am to host a show this year and call it "Throne-room". I believe it is in HIS timing, new season, new assignments.

115

> *"Where the Spirit does not work with the hand there is no art."* **Leonardo da Vinci**
>
> *"More important Than a work of art itself is what it will sow . Art can die, a painting can disappear what can't is the seed "* Joan Miro

Be true to yourself, be honest with what you want to say. Throw out that day of sorrow and release that seed of hope. Sow it into another. When I teach I say there are no mistakes, only-opportunities to grow and stretch and shift. To problem solve and move forward. Each creation, each expression establishes a vision or emotion and captures it in time. Be the seed that says you're not alone or things will get better. There's transformation for the eye of the beholder. Even in the small things there's beauty all around us even in the rubble.

Let's inspire to dig deeper to go higher. I want to speak to those breaking out of their shells testing their wings and just believing they can fly. We are getting kicked out of our nests and it is time to launch. Sometimes we sit on our ideas or dreams waiting for them to hatch. Sometimes we have to protect the vision, dream or idea so it can grow. Other times it is timing but we have to trust and have courage to know when to take that leap of faith.

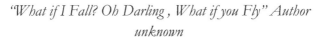

"What if I Fall? Oh Darling , What if you Fly" Author
unknown

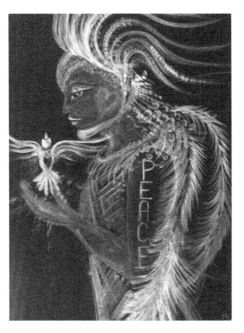

"Hold fast to your dreams for if dreams die, life is a broken winged bird that cannot fly." Author Langston Hughes

So many times our Artistic creations give a voice to the voiceless. It puts a song inside the listener, viewer, observer, watcher, seer.

"A bird doesn't sing because it has an answer, it sings because it has a song" Maya Angelo

I have a love for wings and feathers. They show up in my jewelry and my paintings all the time. As Creators we have certain subjects, certain images that tend to be repeated, refined, revisited and that's okay. There was a whole year or two when I continuously painted hearts. broken hearts, hope filled hearts, hearts on fire, purified hearts. A heart with a white fence falling down (laying down offense) forgiveness and giving it wings to fly. There can be a thousand expressions out of one subject matter. Hundreds of ways to perceive it, express it but when someone sees what you are saying without words that's everything. That's the point of contact, that's a reason to share what you create.

I paint Crowns and Keys and Waves and Lions. Shells and Feathers and Wings. Anchors and Arrows all come together repeating even in my jewelry. These are a few of my favorite things!

I always say, "The Lord knits with a 1000 needles " author unknown.

He pulls things all together till they form a beautiful tapestry of His love. I believe we can use our gifts in the same way. We pull from our history and our vision, it's the view from our hearts. Our hurdles and our hopes and our wilderness places. He pulls together from our dreams and our life experiences which causes us to create one of a kind expressions. We are co-creators and it is inside of us. We are meant and called to share the gifts we've been given. Please know if it is only one person that our creation touches and resonates with then we've accomplished the vision. If the gift has been given and fully received it could inspire others to release their gifts. I'm hoping that's what happens as you read my story but ultimately it is HIS story in us waiting to be launched.

> "He who works with his hands is a laborer. He who works with his hands and his head is a craftsman. He who works with his hands and his head and his heart is an artist." Saint Frances of Assisi

> Just don't give up trying to do what you really want to do. Where there's love and inspiration, I don't think you can go wrong" Ella Fitzgerald

> "The Artist is not a different kind of person , but every person is a different kind of Artist ". Eric Gill

> "In Art there are no mistakes, just a place for redemption. "Jenny Cupp

> *"He will cover you with His feathers. He will shelter you with His wings"* Psalm 91 NLV Bible

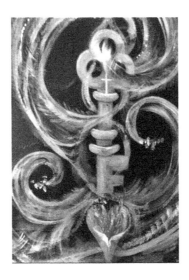

Dictionary definition

CREATOR: Noun

1. A person or thing that brings something into existence.
2. Used as a name for God.

Then God said "Let there be Light"

"Every single human being is created in the image of God; created for dignity, created for kindness, created for mercy." Author Heidi Baker

I ask the Lord every year what is my word for the year ? My word is Flight...Ask Him what is yours and look up the meanings and then I challenge you to create it ..Selah

From the Heart and "For HIS Glory "

Jenny Cupp

Jenny Cupp is a prophetic artist, prophetic voice, and entrepreneur. She is owner and founder of "A Jewel in HIS Crown" she creates one-of- a-kind jewelry designs. Jenny is also a prophetic artist who paints with and for her father, inspirational works of art. Whether painting or making jewelry she finds joy in creating. She does all things for his glory! As the Lord leads, Jenny often releases prophetic words with her paintings. Jenny is a passionate apostolic intercessor and often gathers His like-minded prayer warriors together to bring his presence and Kingdom assignments to the forefront. Jenny champions the arts and is a part of the arts and entertainment mountain. She teaches prophetic art to children and adults. Jenny paints and ministers prophetically at churches and conferences and has traveled and taught in London, Hawaii and YWAM in Australia and throughout the United States. Her form of worship is during worship, she collaborates with the worshippers and with the King of Kings. Her passion is to teach the holiness of his presence through worship and her paintbrushes. Jenny loves to encourage others to birth out their God-given gifts for His Glory. Jenny is currently working on launching a website titled "A Jewel in HIS Crown" offering Prophetic Jewelry, Prophetic paintings, Prints. Clothing, Accessories and Greeting Cards.

Jenny's true passion is for us to use the gifts we've been given to glorify His name...King Jesus "

DEAD END:
WRECK OR BE WRECKED

Nadia S. Alli

Ever wondered what is hindering you from living a luxurious life or why you always feel as if there is always something that is either missing or needs mending?

Finances? Lack of planning strategies? Ignorance? Maybe Mother nature? Reluctance to learn, perhaps? Who knows. If you are expecting to hear something along the lines of "It is because you don't have the resources to become rich" or "You are scared of investing and giving it your all", then I may have to disappoint you on that one.

The answer is ingrained in your thoughts and can be realized by simply introspecting. Nevertheless, it can be quite said that you do not know the definition of 'luxury'. While it is the possession of expensive materials and excellent comfort by definition, the world does not entirely accept this explanation. The majority of the world, if asked their view on luxury, would mention magnificent wealth and a life of bed of roses; how much would say health and peace? And in that, the answer can evidently be pulled that the reason there is no free luxury to disperse around this world in this day and age is because of the lack of knowledge. In fact, the most crucial luxury that should be ingrained into the heads of the humans of today is that of education.

But, so many twists and turns, what exactly is it aimed at?

None, but the one and only Global Crisis - Climate Change.

It simmers down to one question: How aware are we of the ongoing Climatic Crisis?

This century is one faced with many challenges, both anthropogenic and natural, and there is no profound contemplation as to whether or not this requires much thought, as it is definitely not a hoax. While there are a number of issues that are competing on the stage for the spotlight, the Climate Crisis has managed to earn the award. With each passing day, this issue is worsened in a way that is powerfully damaging and disrespectful, all owing to the dominating genesis — *Homo sapiens.*

For the sake of a clear picture, Earth's climate has always been changing, and it is completely natural, but in this era, there is something exceptional about how it is changing. Since the period of industrial revolution, mankind pursuits have been a driving force in making climatic conditions shift from worse to worst, at a rate which is faster than nature planned. While this phenomenon has been realized by quite a lot at least, the concept of what needs to be done to take the edge off is not something that is generally conceptualized.

Though this issue had vividly presented itself initially, there was no room for heed or actions. Rather, leaders and corporatism, who have had (and still have) the most substantial say of course, chose to give priority to power of the purse, while leaving the safety and best interests of man behind. And now, for the moment of truth, the world currently stands at a point approaching the edge, moving at a rate of that faster than a speeding rocket ship defying gravity, such that, once reached, there will be no turning back.

It was realized that trying to fight the issue of Climate Change is useless without an understanding of what it is as well as the cognizance of its intensity. As such, this Chapter seeks to explain and disseminate the awareness of Climate Change from various dimensions in the simplest way possible while simultaneously aiming to create a green economy and simultaneously reducing our carbon footprint. To begin with, the wisdom to realize that there is no life without healthy nature is essential. But the real question is: Is our imperative nature healthy? Well, it is most evidently not and one does not have to look too far to see the collapse of its contingents; from earthly ruination to boundless health jeopardies.

Realizing that the famous crisis of Climate Change is here to stay, certainly for an immensely long time and only an exceptionally small portion of its contributing factors stem from natural and uncontrollable events, the major foundation of its existence must not be disregarded. But, why speak of Climate Change so passionately and holding remotely no touch of regards for humans in this context? Rule number one, the Cause of the Climate Crisis must never be swept under the carpet or nullified in any way.

So, what exactly is climate change is the question you ask?

Well, when last have you seen news or a social media post on heat waves, drought, mass flooding, wildfires or any other such? Probably no longer than last week? This is Climate Change in the least descriptive way possible and it is here to degrade our way of life, steal our peace, and threaten us, leaving us worried for our children's children. It is to no surprise that these subverting occurrences are brutal just as it is certain that it will not leave any part of this Planet unsparred. As you begin to brainstorm, you may think that you do not experience catastrophic wildfires or intense snow-storms but the reality is you may be frazzled by the heat each day or are infuriated about your laundry not drying due to unusually intense or frequent rainfall.

The results of Climate Change have taken a toll on the lives of many from all possible dimensions — health, wealth, safety, livelihood. Declining water supplies, increased health issues and decreased agricultural yields are all major concerns which inflict considerable concerns for us as humans. But...what if I told you that you play a major role in making these disasters occur? What if I tell you the problem revolves around everything you do in your day-to-day life? Oh well, any other vehemence than belief would be absurd.

Do you drive short distances instead of walking or cycling? Do you routinely buy bottled water? Do you depend on shops and stores to provide you with polythene bags upon making a purchase? Do you indulge unnecessarily in processed foods and meat? Do you utilize social media for exclusively sharing your life events?

Yes? Then I have some bad news, you are a tremendous contributor to the Climate Crisis.

This factuality has been accepted worldwide by the most intellectual and there is no question as to whether it should be cross-examined or not.

> *"Scientists have no doubt that humans are causing global warming." — Ilissa Ocko, Climate Scientist*

It's effects on us?

Climate Change means to me what is intended to be reiterated in a modified fashion — luxury deprivation. It means to me everything that it has already modeled itself to be and it means to me the need for awareness and education on this crucial concept. The effects of this event has pushed me to realize that taking care of our planet is not a fancy, it is a need. As an individual with high sensitivity towards living deities, I am extremely sympathetic to the pain and suffering of others along with the elements that sustain us human beings. Climate change impacts us for the negative, inflicting a number of challenging adversities which includes the imposition of health threats, higher costs of living and elevated mental health issues. It impacts me greatly in knowing that in a few years, life will be characterized by many altered changes. It takes peace away as limitless thoughts consume me. The thought that our health in the future will be compromised. The fear that we will be living with expectations of disasters without season. The imagination that all beautiful destinations will no longer be what it currently is. And I know that when I say this, I speak on behalf of many, dwelling in all regions of the globe and it is evidenced below.

"In a 2020 survey, more than half of Americans reported feeling anxious about the climate's impact on their mental health, and more than two-thirds said they were anxious about how climate change would affect the planet.

> *Almost 40 percent of young people say they are hesitant about having children. If nature feels this unmoored today, some ask, why bring children into an even grimmer future?" — The New York Times, United States*

> *"Over half (57%) of child and adolescent psychiatrists surveyed in England are seeing children and young people distressed about the climate crisis and the state of the environment." — Royal College of Psychiatrists, London, England*

> *"Australians are 3 times more worried about climate change than COVID. A mental health crisis is looming." — The Conversation, Australia*

With every line being read, the dominating wonder must be "How can a petty issue like Climate Change have such a significant impact?".

A wake up call: Have you checked how many polar bears are left in the world? Have you checked how many farmers die each year to suicide linked to Climate Change? Have you checked the standing of the global economy?

The disappearance of the Arctic sea ice, rising sea levels, persistent wildfires and acidification of oceans is no coincidence. The basis of these catastrophic events is solely here because of us — humans. We indulge in transportation without regard to distance, we support the wrong companies, we fail to speak up and take actions, we burn the notorious fossil fuels for energy; that is, gas, oil and coal which incorporated solar and decomposing processes some three hundred million years ago that have been once more brought to light after their dreadful discovery in the crust of Earth. This choice of ours, whether natural or led by fear, has cost us severely. Consequently, the unceasing release of greenhouse gasses like carbon dioxide and methane [a product of decaying organic matter] into the air trap heat resulting in the warming of the atmosphere. Emissions from vehicles and motorcycles are considered to be the second largest greenhouse emitter in the world, while fossil fuels' emissions are the ruling cause of global warming. These are the factors that heavily contribute to the infamous global warming and notably, the average global temperature is constantly rising and being embraced rather than prevented, owing to the fact that the increase in burning of fossil fuels is steadily elevating. But again, who is responsible? You and I, in Guyana, in Australia, in South Africa, in the United States, in all terrains of the World.

While our activities play a huge role in handshaking with Climate Change, our cognitive rationale and vocal power must not be underrated. The decisions we make and corporations we support tell who we are and how concerned we are about our lives alongside those of our loved ones. There are numerous reports, evidently available on the internet, which show concern over companies, relaying their level of liability for the astronomical number of emissions produced worldwide. More so, fossil fuels companies are one of the pivotal polluters as they both produce and sell fossil fuel products. This leaves us with the most alarming question: If our Crisis is encouraged by the most powerful entities, how should we move forward in creating a greener economy and a safe environment for our well-being? So much the worse, each region of the world is not affected equally. This simply means that some people are plainly unluckier than others. These individuals happen to hail from low income and now developing countries. Unfair or deserving?

It is, without a doubt, climate change is not a clear-cut subject. There are several myths that are attached to this concern that are vaguely contributing to the climatic chaos. One of the biggest myths lies in the misbelief that trees and plants need carbon dioxide. While this is materially true, the quantity of carbon dioxide they can absorb is finite, and the amount of this production by humans is insurmountable. Another costly misapprehension is that of climate change being a future problem. As emphasized on the fact that knowledge is limited in this respect, it is held in the eyes of many that today's catastrophes are natural with very minimal need to be vigilant at this moment. China being the only country responsible for climate change is another point that falls under this notion. Though it is no fiction that it is one of the largest emitters of carbon emissions in the world, it also presents itself as one of the substantially large investors in renewables. But the point is the reality that emissions hail from different slants of the globe, therefore it is not only China's duty to act.

It is effectively known that climate change made an appearance roughly around the nineteenth century, however, has become worse owing to the bountiful emissions of carbon dioxide. This phenomenon is flawed and the need to relay that there has been natural heating and cooling has indeed occurred, but human executions are making it heat while depriving it of its right to cool must be emphasized.

A world with continued Climate Change will influence every possible dimension of our lives there is: health, safety, food, production, security. Food scarcity, water degradation, poverty, deteriorating health, desertification [fertile lands becoming dried up thereby losing its fertility], heavy and hot air quality, species extinction and biodiversity [flora and fauna] loss will be the new norm. Even worse, the planet will exceed its carrying capacity, resulting in dramatically increased deaths owing to the fact that there will not be enough resources to treat patients and sustain people. A great perspective has been the Covid-19 crisis whereby hospitals in first world countries like the United

States of America ran out of supplies to alleviate patients' sufferings. As a result, some patients succumbed. This only goes to show one thing — that is, demand would always be greater than supply should there be an emergency crisis on our planet, and Covid-19 has exemplified this theory.

To shed some light on recent catastrophes that occurred around the globe, there were the bushfires which took place in Australia in 2019-2020, wildfires in Turkey in 2021, flash floods in Indonesia in 2020 and the extinction of the last male Northern White Rhinoceros.

Although we humans can do the maximum to reduce our climatic issue as much as possible, the reality is that destructive activities are here to stay. Vehicles are acknowledged as one of the leading sources of emissions and subsequently, global warming, but most of the world, especially business bodies are dependent on such for a number of reasons. Besides, for we as mankind, vehicles are convenient and put people in positions to achieve the comfort they crave. Not to mention, not everyone may be able to afford a life where there is great-mass transportation. This puts the tackle on a losing end such that while some people may continue using vehicles by choice, others will do the same for genuine and necessary purposes.

During the pandemic, greenhouse gas emissions and thereafter, air pollution, has reportedly been reduced around the world owing to the fact that there has been restrictions and deaths of employees in the larger portion of the globe's travel arena and industry operation respectively. However, despite this drop, no *major* improvements came to light. In fact, this incident was short-termed and has been insufficient to grow a green economy. This shows how far the crisis has taken off.

Creating a safe and green world will be one of the most challenging goals to achieve at this point, however no hopes should be lost as we, together, can reduce the rate at which Climate Change is accelerating. Solutions to our very own global crisis is as simple as we make it. Taking a step back to introspect our mentality is an ideal way of kick-starting the journey to a safe planet. Our choices and contemporary lifestyle need to first be evaluated and reflected on so as to assess or rather realize its impacts on our environment and the globe at large. We make an insurmountable amount of decisions in our lifetime which have the ability to decide whether or not our planet is safe. If the majority of the population decides that they do not want to entertain climate change, then the planet would stand a great chance of rejuvenating before it reaches the breakdown point. Strategizing to obtain this objective is no tough feat for us consumers, taking into account that corporations are dependent on us to thrive. Hence, if we lay the cards and apply pressure for them to match their principles with ours, they will conform. We must never forget that business entities hold the ability to either make or break the environment.

"Consumerism plays a role too. Most of us are responsible for the demand of the products corporations put out. We contribute to corporate emissions by supporting businesses who emit excessively. We are part of the system. We are all complicit in the actions against our climate. This means it's our responsibility, as the inhabitants of this planet, to take action against it.

> *If we choose to voice ourselves wisely, both in politics and economics, it will help lighten the load of the earth. Research the candidates running in your area and investigate the companies you invest in; find the CEOs and companies whose decisions reflect a belief*

> *in climate change and respect for the environment*
> *and abandon those who don't."*
> *— Hira*

In addition to our vocal actions, we can fulfill nature's wish — to care and be taken care of. In the environmental world, the term 'garbage' is just a word composed of seven letters and is 'meaningless as it deceivingly sounds'. The natural world only recognizes the processes of reusing or recycling but has been robbed of that right as humans have physically insisted that it be an expendable sphere. Think about it. You do not need a plastic straw to drink. Using non-woven polypropylene bags is not a crime. Your empty room does not need lights to survive.

You may be overwhelmed by the thoughts that you have no significant influence over this matter, but the fact is you are not the only one who thinks this way.

> *"It is only one straw — said 8 billion people."*
> *— Anne-Marie Bonneau*

Simply creating the right mindset is crucial in achieving the end goal. Eliminate the thoughts "The Government will deal with it" or "This challenge is too large for me to face, my actions would not make a difference".

Don't you think you are accompanied by souls who share the same view?! Don't you think the world would have been a better place if you were the only one with this thought?

Climate change is one of the biggest undermining barbarities that this era is faced with, threatening our global economy, pressurizing future generations, jeopardizing our health and endangering our lives. Because of its severity and effects, the delay in the span to go green cannot be prolonged any further and action is desperately needed.

> *"Climate change is a global matter. It might have different effects on several countries but nevertheless the changing of our climate is a problem that will influence the whole world. Therefore, several countries will have to cooperate in the battle against climate change. A global problem needs a global solution."*
> — *Bernadet van den Pol*

One of the most captivatingly applicable quotes that is unquestionably intriguing and motivating to the advocacy of fabricating a greener economy was uttered by commendable Zero-waste chef, Anne Marie Bonneau:

"We don't need a handful of people doing zero waste perfectly, we need millions of people doing it imperfectly."

This quote dates back to our mindset and wisdom. As critical as it is, we do not need to perfect the art of lessening our shower period or elapse distances via feet on less luckier days. What is needed is information dissemination. What is needed is unity and a little mindfulness towards our dear Planet. But the preferred 'mode of action' chosen by us citizens of Earth was denial and delay in the direction of destruction.

Now, as we shift to the brighter side of things, the stride in this fight may not yet be one to transport us to the seventh heaven, but there have been tracks carved, preparation made and movements taken to accommodate the battle. The most famous is the Climate Pledge, whose primary goal is to annually reduce 1.98 billion metric tons of carbon emissions by the year 2040. After all has been said and done, Jack must certainly be given his jacket...And because this episode was generalized, it is, at best, ethical to finally deliver the positive, relaxing remarks in the same respect. Though it can safely be said that the larger majority of the business arena have given themselves up to the hands of enjoyment, it is not the same for some, at least, 200 global organizations, inclusive of HP, ASOS, Nespresso and Salesforce, whose signatures are imprinted by blots of ink on the pledging sheet. Whether shocking thoughts are racing in the head or the mind is calmer than glass, these working measures are fortunately and needing supported by some world class companies.

Conclusively, there is still hope for the future because despite Climate Change being caused by us and is our problem, we have the right to choose, the right to speak and the right to decide who to give our money and support to. No nation progresses when its people are divided and of course, mountains are moved at the feet of unity. Besides, everyone will eventually be hurt by Climate Change which is why a collective initiative is urgently needed to combat this issue and ensure the talk is walked. This crisis is ours to solve, it is our responsibility and the sooner we own it, the better for us all, so let us vow to leave an empty seat for duty, wisdom and respect while being mindful of what John Dickinson said best: United we stand, Divided we Fall.

This leaves us with the final questions: Are we doing anything today to sustain our environment? Are we willing to make lifestyle changes? Or do we really want to welcome TEOTWAWKI?

Nadia Alli hails from Guyana, South America, where she spent all her life thus far, and is an Undergraduate Student at the University of Guyana. During her early years, she was skilled in writing and it did not take her long to realize that. In fact, she was often commended by well-experienced teachers for her exceptional essays. At age 9, out of boredom, she stapled a few typing papers together and made it into a book-like object, after which she proceeded to collate some words on. In approximately thirty minutes, a creative short story with visualizations and a book-cover was assembled.

As years progressed, Nadia did not see it feasible to take this aptitude of hers to the next level, and as such, she steered into another direction, but her love for writing remained unwavering. While in a totally new arena of studying the Sciences at University, Nadia was compelled to pursue courses that entailed nothing of her pivotal focus. Nevertheless, this experience resulted in her developing a passion for social change and subsequently converted her into a social activist, leading to one of the most powerful combinations; a skill at writing and a desire for social change; a bond which continues to consolidate with each passing day.

After many mind-altering experiences, Nadia has eventually grown to realize that her true field of purpose lies within medicine. She believes in pursuing what she loves without fear or brakes. Nevertheless, though Nadia is resolutely chasing after a career in medicine which she is deeply spirited about, she has decided to put her talent of writing into a noble use with hopes of her voice being impactful through words. She wishes to use her passion for change, whether it is writing or medicine; all for the betterment of us, all for the betterment of the world.

Contact info:
Name: Nadia Sara Alli
Address: 151 Railway View, Meten-Meer-Zorg, West Coast Demerara, Georgetown, Guyana, South America.
Phone number: +592 6645566
Email: nadiagy01@gmail.com
Instagram: @nadiaalli_

ONE LITTLE STEP IS A STEP CLOSER

Emily Oppong-Dwamena

I often remember my excitement for summer as a kid, and how much I dreaded winter. How can you blame me? It's summer break from school, trips to the beach, dresses for three months straight, and most importantly the hours of sun. Every kid's happy place. This same cycle of happiness and sadness continued up until I reached high school. I had no longer been a kid since everything was now changing. My path in high school is really the path to the rest of my life.

My first year of high school was great timing with the pandemic. I felt my personality had been stripped away from me. I was more shy, dreaded school, and lacked confidence. With the pandemic, I did not leave my house often. Instead, I would find ways not to leave my house, which included virtual school. This being my sophomore year, I needed to put in effort to sustain decent grades. I was confused why I suddenly lacked motivation and was always sad during the late fall and whole of winter. Even my hair started to fall out. I did research and discovered a common condition of Seasonal Affective Disorder (SAD).

This condition made perfect sense to me. SAD is a depression that occurs at the same time each year due to the lack of sunlight in some climates. Additionally, it is a subtype to Major Depressive disorder and Bipolar disorder; people will experience symptoms of these disorders only during the late Fall and whole of Winter. I was shocked to hear this as a common condition. I felt more comfortable knowing I was not the only one suffering from this. In fact, SAD is four times more likely to appear in women than men. With SAD, there is an increase in sleep, appetite, and weight. It can be hard dealing with this disorder since it is deemed not socially acceptable. Many people receive negative feedback when dealing with depressive disorders since it is "dramatic" or fortunate people "should not have a reason to be sad." It is important that many who suffer from this, especially young teen girls, learn to support each other and feel comfortable expressing themselves without the possibility of judgment.

Why am I handing you this anecdote? Well, it brings the idea of Climate Change. With Climate Change, there is a long term battle of weather patterns; temperature rises. Hotter weather may seem like a good outcome, however, the problem is what we, humans, are doing to make this happen and why it is such a problem.

Climate change not only impacts me but it also impacts the rest of the world. Some regions may experience more rainfall droughts, rise in temperatures, or wilder weather, all of which are symptoms of climate change As much as we enjoy warm climates, it is not something we desire in the Winter. The rise in temperature could be limiting our years on earth.

Don't you want to create a future for yourself? With our current status on climate change, the future is unforeseeable. Not only are we impacting current society, but future generations too.

Let's debunk a few misconceptions of climate change, according to UCL News: "climate change is just part of the cycle." Yes it is true climate changes frequently, however, there is no naturality. Climate change reacts to the amount of greenhouse gasses emitted. Furthermore, "A study using 700 climate records showed that, over the last 2,000 years, the only time the climate all around the World has changed at the same time and in the same direction has been in the last 150 years, when over 98% of the surface of the planet has warmed" (UCL News).

Next, we often hear "Carbon Dioxide does not have a significant effect since it is a small part of the atmosphere." This misconception is common. But, any amount of carbon dioxide can increase the road to climate change, simply because it's a greenhouse gas.

Lastly, "climate changes because of sunspots." Although sunspots can alter temperature, there is no immense trend. Sunspots have not made a recent impact, showing it cannot be a reason for global warming.

After researching more on climate change, I came across a well-known activist. Known for her youth yet powerful influence, Greta Thunberg. You either know this name or you do not. Personally, she inspires me, along with other teenagers globally. After becoming an activist at 12 years old, she has managed to make more history than many today.

Greta once said, "We can't save the world by playing by the rules. Because the rules have to be changed." These words alone show her passion for this topic. Despite the bullying she faces because of her disease, Asperger's, a type of autism, she keeps herself strong. With her school strike for climate, Greta motivated others in her efforts to meet carbon emissions targets. This let many individuals organize strikes of their own.

Greta recommends we leave fossil fuels in the ground. This would completely transform the current economy. Without doing so, we could be eliminating our time on Earth. This brings us to the topic of the Carbon Budget.

What is the carbon budget? It is Carbon Dioxide emissions committed over a period of time. With Greta's beliefs. She wants to limit the amount of carbon dioxide emissions committed. This may sound easy, however, many factors come into play such as decomposition, ocean release, and respiration. Human activities that prevent this are cement production, deforestation, fossil fuels, and oil and natural gasses.

Climate change plays a role in the current pandemic. It is no secret we have been fighting this pandemic for the last few years. Climate change only makes matters worse with the spread of pathogens. This is because when the planet begins to get hotter, people are seeking to find the coolest possible environments, increasing human contact. The reason being, Deforestation.

What is Deforestation? "Loss of habitat forces animals to migrate and potentially contact other animals or people and share germs" according to Harvard School of Public Health. Just as important, places with poorer air conditions are more likely to contract covid- 19. The contaminated air increases the chances of sickness and can even kill people. The covid-19 pandemic has only made matters worse for climate change. People are able to contract illnesses due to the unclean air quality.

My C, climate change, has recently played a role in the ongoing forest fires in California, USA. Although I do not live there, many entertainment influencers I follow live there and are greatly impacted by these fires. Because of the overheating of plants in forests, it is more likely to cause wildfires. In fact, *The New York Times* reported research saying "the number of fires could increase by about 20 percent or more by the 2040s, and that the total burned area could increase by about 25 percent or more" and "short events like heat waves impact fire" says Aurora A. Gutierrez, a researcher at the University of California Irvine. The problem with these fires is that adults and children are being harmed. Not only has climate change harmed the environment, individuals are being taken away, along with their homes. Many people are having to seek shelter away from the fire.

Another role the wildfires play is destroying land for organisms living in forests. With the release of air pollution, the contaminated air produces health risks. Health risks like lung cancer, heart disease, and respiratory infections are developed. Although wildlife may show less significance to the economy, they are just as harmed. Many fail to realize we need wildlife to keep ecosystems functioning, and to survive off food. When wildlife is destroyed, we slowly suffer.

Anyone can make a difference and prevent climate change. This can be as simple as limiting your traveling, limiting electricity, and watching the food we eat. Although I am only 16 years old, I want to make a difference with climate change. I could campaign, fundraise, even start a worldwide petition. I care for wildlife, individuals impacted by wildfires, and contracted illnesses. One little step is a step closer to a happier and more beautiful world. We cannot take the earth for granted.

https://www.hsph.harvard.edu/c-change/subtopics/coronavirus-and-climate-change/

https://www.nytimes.com/2021/11/17/climate/climate-change-wildfire-risk.html#:~:text=The%20research%2C%20which%20examined%20daily,about%2025%20percent%20or%20more.

https://www.ucl.ac.uk/news/2019/sep/analysis-five-climate-change-science-misconceptions-debunked

https://medlineplus.gov/genetics/condition/seasonal-affective-disorder/

My name is Emily Oppong-Dwamena. I am currently in 12th grade attending East Brunswick High School in East Brunswick, New Jersey. I am part of many clubs such as National Honors Society, English Honors Society, Spanish Honors Society, Family, Career and Community Leaders of America (FCCLA), and Student Council, which I plan to run for Vice President next school year. Outside of school, I play field hockey during the fall, and do track and field in the Winter and Spring. I have been doing both sports since 8th grade and plan to continue my track profession at college. I also volunteer with the Youth Council, a volunteer program provided in my town. I am a huge music lover. My favorite art of music is R & B. I used to play the violin in elementary school and I am currently self-taught in piano. I grew up in a household with my parents, and three siblings, me being the youngest. As the youngest, I like to think of myself as the most destined for success. With my interest in psychology and healthcare, I plan to be a forensic psychiatrist in the future. Being part of this book allows me to express my creativity and activism toward the topic of climate change. My goal with this book is to alert the public of the current circumstances we are facing so we can do our best to prevent them.

The Promise of Affluence

IS A PROMISE OF CHANGE

Landra Richards

We are dire but **NOT HOPELESS.**

As a science teacher at Success Academy, I have bumped into brilliantly curious scholars who question and call out the idea of acting on climate change when we are already "too far gone" and no satisfactory operative solution seems to fix it. Such remarks from children ages 10-13 are always momentarily mind-boggling to me, but it is thought-provoking and challenges my tendencies of confirmation bias. There is a need to understand why youths would believe any act of change now would be futile for future progression. I began to realize that they feel as though individual responsibility has no abstract effect on climate change, a matter that demands global & collective responsibility. That is a fair point, but believing in a zero social-action motive is the first blunder people make when approaching this global phantom. Young people are developing the mindset that they have to wait until they hold a position of "political leadership" before they can make mass changes that tackle climate change. Inevitably they would understandably concur with the thought that collective responsibility overrides individual responsibility when handling massive issues. This is far from the truth. The problem begins from a personal stance of you looking into your own inadequacies.

Like the story of the little bird and the forest fire shared among the Aztec people of Mexico..... If you are capable of building yourself into a more powerful individual & do a tremendous amount of good not just for yourself but the people in your immediate surroundings as well, then you are capable of expanding your competence. Your level of competence will allow you to take place in your community as an effective leader. As an **effective leader**, you are then capable of avoiding unwise choices when making collective political decisions that will create impactful alterations on a larger scale. So if we don't have our own personal space in order we can't go about reorganizing the world, the promise of change -*affluence*- has to begin with individual responsibility.

...

"It's one man for himself and gone for us all!" a debatably malicious statement with subjective meaning that my 6th-grade teacher, Dr. Ngwenya, reiterated to us, his students, in "dire situations", like exams and competitions. It somehow resonates with the idea of individuality and lonesomeness despite being surrounded by a plethora of individuals under the same pressure. It made us feel as though we were all in it alone however, this should never be the case when dealing with climate change. Climate change is not a one-man's crisis. Many of you may have experienced this a few times in your day-to-day life, and the same can be said about how we are processing and choosing to find global solutions for climate change. The outcome of dire situations had been magnified during the first few months of the COVID-19 pandemic, where everyone was in a similar circumstance, passing by with their left fist behind their back clinching to self-interest, and their right, snatching whatever they could get. Many of us felt this lonesomeness and the need to come first because we didn't know what would happen next. Adhering to precautions of isolation, limited contact, masks, and vaccines as the best solution lead an economy built off of networking, transport, and physical rendezvous to cascade.

Acknowledging there is no solution to climate change leaves you reading every report with caution. Over the years of reading and understanding climate change, you begin to question how reliable climate change projections are.

There first was an assessment from the Intergovernmental Panel on Climate Change (IPCC), a United Nations-created multinational body of scientists. It discovered that global temperatures have been rising for decades, that man-made emissions are the primary reason, atmospheric concentrations were reported to be the greatest in 800,000 years, and that the consequences included rising sea levels, melting glaciers, and increased heat waves.

Then came the United States National Climate Assessment, a study by 300 U.S. scientists that was even scarier than the IPCC report. It begins, "Climate change, formerly thought to be a distant future concern, has pushed firmly into the present." Americans are already suffering as a result of global warming. Floods are more common; wildfires are more difficult to manage; and rainstorms are more intense. Naturally, climate skeptics criticized the claims. According to Paul Knappenberger and Patrick Michaels of the Cato Institute, a libertarian think tank, the data was inflated, cherry-picked, or both. Consider a contrary study led by a Harvard scholar, they suggested that heat-related mortality have decreased in 105 U.S. cities during the late 1980s.

The contradictions and unreliability of the measurement magnifies with time progression. Because the data provided is used again in future research projects, this becomes an accumulation of inaccuracies over time. The error bars around these projections become so wide that we won't be able to measure the positive or negative effects of anything we do as of now. With an accumulation of these errors how can we measure the consequences of our actions? Besides that, what is the solution? It's a more complex situation of trial and error.

Greta Thomas protests that it is unfair; the generation that has birthed us into this new era has passed down their global disputes and conflicts and look to us for solutions. The dreams of youth as well as their childhood have been stolen with the empty words of chivalrous dialogues on money and fairy tales of eternal economic growth as we chip into the age of extinction.

Increase child nutrition enough to improve the development and physiology directed towards brain power.

Jordan Peterson, when asked if climate change is an issue that can lead to global unity, moving us beyond debates of C16 where humanity can discover its global map of meaning, replied "NO". His history of delving into UN committees sustainable economic and ecological development and relevant literature lead him to the idea that climate change is a catastrophic mess and the idea that it will unite the globe is bizarre. It's difficult to separate science from politics and if the more radical claims were true there was no definite action for it.

Germany tried wind and solar. It produced more CO2 than when it started because they had to turn on the coal fire plants again.

Cutting back? Maybe, except data shows that if we can get the GDP of the entire population of about 5k a year and then they start caring about the event a perfectly strong case and humane one because the idea would lead to tackling the idea of poverty. Increased consumption in the short term and they would start caring about the event and things would clear up.

Leon Lomburg took the un millennium goals, 200 goals isn't a plan Jordan describes this as a wish list. There is a need for prioritization. But it's difficult to do so because each goal has its constituents, and it would irritate the constituents but without prioritization, implementation becomes inconceivable. Lombart gathered a group of economists to help resolve this, they ranked the order of development goals in terms of their returns on investment and presented a final list in which addressing global warming was shockingly not on the list. He wrote a book "how to spend 75 billion dollars to make the world a better place ". Almost everything recommended had to do with increased child nutrition within developing countries.

No single solution can solve all problems.

LANDRA ANATHA RICHARDS

I am a 19 year old final year undergraduate at the University of Guyana, pursuing a Bachelor's Degree in Biology to better understand biodiversity and how we influence it's change for the better. I have been blessed as a multipotentialite so my passion lies in multiple aspects of life.

I am a co-editor and co-creator of the M.O.V.E. (Mangrove Operations and Volunteer Equities) in Guyana. A fourth year representative of the University of Guyana Bio Club, a personal yoga instructor/trainer for kids, an athlete, artist, writer and model at Traits Management.

My goal is to service myself and others by caring for the earth and its inhabitants. More specifically I aim to become an animal rehabilitator and a teacher to whoever is willing to lend an ear.

Made in the USA
Middletown, DE
14 October 2023

40588283R00089